RAVE REVIEWS FOR

SATISFACTION
GUARANTEED™

And now the book, based upon "Six Star Customer Satisfaction"

"Brian is the Norman Vincent Peale of Customer Service."
Debbie Wagner, Systems Professional – Ford Motor Company

"Brian Lee has a fantastic message for everyone. Every employer should take advantage of the wonderful opportunity to present this book, "Satisfaction Guaranteed," as a personal copy to each and every employee."
Lyle Manery, CLU, CH.F.C – Chimo Financial Services Inc.

"Brian Lee's customer satisfaction message will change how you look at the world; both in the workplace and your personal life. You rock, Brian!"
Travis Shand, Promotions – WIC TV

"The Mess Up, Fess Up, Dress Up approach to customer service is just one of many breakthrough concepts that makes "Satisfaction Guaranteed" a must-read for any organization that wants to increase referrals and sales."
Lou Schizas, President – Queens Capital Corporation

"You far exceeded my expectations and you have delivered more than you promised."
Bob Hefferman, V.P. Customer Service – The Dial Corp.

A

MORE RAVE REVIEWS FOR *B*RIAN LEE'S

SATISFACTION GUARANTEED™

"Book publishers always guarantee satisfaction. Now they have a paint-by-the-numbers manual to provide guidance and justify their actions. Highly Recommended."

Dan Poynter – The Self-Publishing Manual

"To survive in today's challenging and demanding marketplace, we need dynamic, competitive employees dedicated to meeting our customers' expectations. Your "Six Star" secrets gave us that edge."

G.J. Reddington, President – Sears

"Your "Six Star" message has profoundly changed the way our people perform their jobs."

Mitch Regiec, FPCM President – Canadian Society of Club Managers

"Your "Six Star" values is the most valuable education program I have ever seen."

Peter Howard, President – O.H.I. (G.M., Chateau Laurier)

"By suggesting that innkeepers perceive their businesses from a customers' point of view, you offered them new ideas and have given us much food for thought."

Sandra LaRuffa, Executive Director –
Bed & Breakfast Innkeepers of Northern California

B

SATISFACTION GUARANTEED™

Satisfy Every Customer Every Time

Master the Six Secrets of How to Create
World-Class Customer Satisfaction

Brian C. Lee CSP
Canada's "Mr. Enthusiasm"

ISBN 0–921328–02–8
(PB600)/DT#13/08/15/96

Published by Mastery Publishing
(a Division of Custom Learning Systems Group Ltd.)
#200, 2133 Kensington Road N.W.
Calgary, Alberta T2N 3R8
Phone: (403) 245–2428 Fax: (403) 228–6776
Toll Free: 1–800–66–SPEAK
Email: info@customlearning.com
Web site: www.customlearning.com

First Edition 1996 by Brian Lee CSP

1. Customer Service   2. Business Improvement
Copyright 1996   Edition #19 - 08/29/05

Printed and bound in Canada

C

D

$\mathcal{P}$ROFILE OF AN AUTHOR AND WORLD-CLASS PROFESSIONAL SPEAKER

$\mathcal{B}$RIAN LEE CSP

Active as a public speaker from the age of 15 when he completed a Junior Achievement course, Brian Lee CSP has applied his exceptional communications skills in a host of ways.

Authored by Brian Lee CSP
"Mr. Customer Satisfaction"
Canada's "Mr. Enthusiasm"

Becoming successful in business as the Vice-President of a major retail firm by the age of 25, he then entered politics two years later and was elected Calgary's youngest-ever Alderman. Nine productive years in public life on City Council and as a Provincial MLA provided Brian with public speaking opportunities on a daily basis.

Brian Lee's Career Highlights

◆ Brian Lee is a past president of the Canadian Association of Professional Speakers (Alberta Chapter) and past Assistant Area Governor, Toastmasters International as well as past president of the University of Calgary Oxford Debating Society.

◆ Brian Lee CSP is one of North America's leading experts in the field of World-Class Customer Satisfaction and Change Leadership has authored five books.

◆ For two consecutive years, Brian has been evaluated by the International Customer Service Association Conference as the number one rated Customer Service Speaker in the world.

◆ "Mr. Customer Satisfaction" travels over 150,000 miles a year, delivering over 180 keynotes and seminars, and has spoken in every state and province, and 12 countries worldwide.

◆ As both a speaker and implementation consultant to over 100 Fortune 500 corporations and health care organizations, Brian is sought-after as an advisor/coach to senior management, specializing in long-term strategic solutions.

◆ He has been awarded the National Speakers Association Professional Designation, CSP (Certified Speaking Professional), becoming one of less than 20 in Canada, and 500 in the world.

◆ Custom Learning Systems Group Ltd. (CLS) was founded by Brian Lee CSP in 1984. Headquartered in Calgary, Alberta, CLS has offices in Winnipeg and Toronto, and serves its client roster of 6,000 organizations in North America with a team of 24 world-class trainers and communication professionals.

Put Brian Lee to work for your next conference or meeting.
1-800-66-SPEAK (667-7325) • Keynotes • Seminars • Consulting • Coaching
(for information, see Customer Responsiveness/Professional Development page 109)

E

F

ACKNOWLEDGEMENTS

The following individuals are gratefully acknowledged for their contribution, encouragement and support:

- ◆ Valerie Cade Lee
- ◆ Grant McGinnes
- ◆ Dan Poynter
- ◆ Margo Lee
- ◆ Tom Peters
- ◆ Pat Goodberry-Dyck
- ◆ Bruce Lee
- ◆ Kelly Rose
- ◆ Sue Krawchuk

- ◆ Aime Tetrault
- ◆ Roy Friedman
- ◆ Lyle Manery, CLU, CH.F.C.
- ◆ Ken Cade
- ◆ Lou Schiza
- ◆ Cec Hanec
- ◆ Candis McLean
- ◆ Nicole Hofferd

H

SATISFACTION GUARANTEED™

How to Satisfy Every Customer Every Time

This book is based upon Brian Lee's acclaimed "Six Star™" Customer Satisfaction seminar series, with over 500,000 graduates in the past 14 years. Mastery Publishing Co. is publishing the complete series in book form. Other titles in the series are:

- **Winning With Difficult Customers**

  How You Can Say to the Most Difficult Customer in the World ... "Come and Get Me!"

- **Stress-Free Service Excellence**

  How to Create a Stress–free Environment for Your Customers and You

- **One Minute S.E.R.V.I.C.E. Selling**

  How to Gain a Competitive Advantage by Helping Others Get What They Want

- **Managing Moments of Truth**

  How to Continuously Improve Customer Satisfaction

- **Self-Esteem and Service Superstars**

  How to Enhance Self-Esteem for Improved Service Excellence

I

J

Satisfaction Guaranteed™

The Six Values of Lifetime Customer Loyalty

K

$\mathscr{F}$OREWARD

"The whole secret to success in business is to do
or know something that nobody else does."
– Aristotle Onassis

$\mathcal{E}$xcellence. It's a noble pursuit, but finding it in customer service can be tough.

I'd been travelling into Sault Ste. Marie, Ontario for several months, planning to do a series of seminars. The Sault was a typical Canadian border city in the 1990s and all I heard was doom and gloom.

Practically every business person I talked to said "government" should take action, "government" should rescind the Canada/U.S. Free Trade Agreement, and "government" should make it illegal for anyone to cross the border and purchase products on the other side in Sault Ste. Marie, Michigan.

Crossborder shopping in Canada, like outshopping in the United States, is a major issue. It will probably always be one.

When I was speaking in Provost, Alberta, I found out they were worried about their people shopping in Wainwright. When I was in Wainwright, I heard people there who were worried about losing customers to Edmonton. In Edmonton, they worry about people going across the line into the United States. Canada worries about the U.S. and the U.S. worries about Canada.

It's an epidemic.

1

The statistics in Sault Ste. Marie were pretty typical, with the average resident spending about $700 a year shopping in Michigan.

Merchants on the Canadian side were livid.

In the midst of all this gloom and doom, in the middle of tough times, as bad as things apparently were, every time I drove past a grocery store called Loeb's IGA the parking lot was full.

As a matter of fact, when I asked who was good in customer service in Sault Ste. Marie, as I do everywhere I go, the people said, "Loeb's IGA."

I asked my hosts to introduce me to the owners, Judy and Larry Cairns.

"How's business?" I asked, and they said, "Great! As a matter of fact, it's up 30 percent."

Hmm. Up 30 percent? When the whole town is headed south? What gives?

I said, "How are you doing on prices?"

They said, "We're competitive."

I said, "Are you the lowest on everything?"

They said, "No, we're competitive."

I said, "Could you give me a tour?"

They said, "We'd be delighted."

Now I didn't need a tour to see the former Greyhound bus in the parking lot, painted over with "Loeb's IGA" on the side. It is used to pick up senior citizens twice a week and bring them to the store; the bag boys even ride back with them to carry the groceries to their front door.

Nice touch.

I didn't need a tour to see how clean the store was and how user-friendly everything seemed to be. There were plants everywhere. When I came in the front door, I noticed something that took me all the way back to my high school days when I worked at Safeway in Calgary.

Back then, if a customer dared ask to use the phone, we'd make him or her go in the back, over the boxes, past the smelly bathrooms, over the bottle depot, to the telephone – it was a major imposition on our lives.

At Loeb's, there is a telephone in the front entrance facing you as you come in. It's as if they wanted you to use it.

In Sault Ste. Marie, almost everyone was buying dairy products on the American side because it was supposed to be so much cheaper, but at

2

Loeb's IGA they had a sign up above their cheese that said, "We will slice it, dice it, grate it, you name it, we'll do it."

User-friendly.

However, the acid test for a food store – if you are the one who buys the groceries in your house, you'll know – comes every Saturday afternoon. When the store is jam-packed with shoppers, how long do you wait to get through the checkout line and on your way?

At Loeb's, the answer is no more than two carts per line any day of the week. Period.

Now those of you who do the scheduling at your place of business know that this is a pretty demanding expectation. They meet it at Loeb's every Saturday.

How was it, I had to ask, that they had created this oasis of customer service excellence in the midst of a wasteland?

The answer was music to my ears.

"Brian," they said, "we went to a seminar three years ago and the speaker said, 'Consider the customer in everything you do.' "

Exactly!

Now Loeb's IGA did three critical things uniquely different.

First, they got educated. They learned something about customer service. Second, they trained all their people in what they had learned. Third, they acted on that knowledge – immediately.

That's what Six Star Customer Satisfaction is all about!

The key to success, whether you are an owner, a manager, a front-line associate, an entrepreneur, or whether you work in government, or private business, or in the non-profit sector, is about how you can create a career advantage for yourself, personally, and do well regardless of how the economy is doing. As a matter of fact, you will grow in spite of hard times.

If you will take my challenge to get educated and put this knowledge to work in your industry, in your career, in your working life; if you will utilize the most powerful advancement tool – Total Customer Satisfaction – you too, can gain the competitive advantage that Loeb's IGA has.

By the way, there were five stores operating in a six-block radius of Loeb's IGA in Sault Ste. Marie and another one had just closed because they couldn't take the heat.

Wouldn't you like to be the Loeb's IGA of your market/profession?

3

Foreward

Just "D.O. I.T." Checklist

Recommendations:

❏ 1. Conduct a "best practises" tour and visit the three organizations in your market area that are famous for "world-class" customer satisfaction. Ask a lot of questions.

❏ 2. Invest in yourself. Take a minimum of 18 hours a year in Customer Service-related training.

❏ 3. Whatever inspires you in this book, act on it URGENTLY. Ideas have a way of "cooling down" over time.

$\mathcal{W}$HAT IS CUSTOMER SERVICE?

BOLD GOALS:
"Whatever you can do or dream you can do, begin it.
Boldness has genius, power, and magic in it."

$\mathcal{R}$uss is irritated. He's a friend of mine who lives in Boulder, Colorado, and like many of you, he's tired of bad service. Have you ever noticed that people will take your money and never even look at you? Russ has. He claims it is now his prime goal in life to get a retail clerk to thank him (or say "please") when he makes a purchase.

If somebody won't even look at him when he pays for goods or services he just holds onto his money with a firm grip until the clerk looks him squarely in the eye – usually like he's unbalanced or something – and then, in the most obvious of voices, he says, "Thaaaaannnnk you."

What is service? A good definition is:
"Adding you to your product or services."

It's almost as if you have to beg to be thanked.

My friend Barry, in Houston, told me he was in a store buying something and he said to the clerk, "You didn't smile and you didn't say thank you."

The clerk's reply? "It's on your receipt."

Have we sunk so low?

Stanley Marcus, the founder of the Neiman-Marcus department store chain said, "Customers are people. Consumers are statistics."

So true.

I believe the Consumers Association should drop that name and call itself the Customers Association because we are all customers. I think ultimately what we all aspire to as customers is to be treated as individuals.

What is service? Well a good definition is, "*Adding you to your product or services.*"

Almost all of us own a car. No matter what car company you've purchased from in the last few years, there are literally thousands and thousands of people whose efforts have gone into building that automobile.

There are designers and engineers and assembly people. There are accountants and managers and quality control people. Yet, who had the most impact on how you view that manufacturer? Probably the salesperson.

The irony of it all is that the car salesperson is the least-trained of the entire chain. The average car salesperson lasts about eight months and only about one-third make a decent living. You're no doubt aware of his suspect reputation among the buying public, of his image best represented by Kurt Russell in the film, "Used Cars." You know, bad plaid.

How many companies blow it all by having minimum wage employees, with little or no training, dealing directly with the customer?

The reason I got elected to city council as the youngest alderman in Calgary's history was not because I was wealthy and it certainly wasn't because I was smart. No, it was because I was prepared to knock on 11,000 doors in just four weeks.

And people say to me, "Brian, how did you do that?"

One door at a time.

It was kind of a waste of time knocking on doors and having nobody answer, so I would have campaign workers going up and down the street getting people to come out to meet me.

I would say to them, "Look, when you knock on that door, you are me. As far as those people are concerned, their perception of you is their perception of me."

It's the same with your business, government department or non-profit organization. The public's perception of your organization is their perception of you, one at a time. It is very much a personal thing.

6

If that car salesperson knew nothing about the car he was trying to sell you, or if he was rude or indifferent or smelled bad, how would you feel about the company he represented?

The Japanese phrase for customer service means,
"Honoured visitor in one's house."

My friend Ed in Atlanta was interested in a particular automobile that retailed for around $30,000. He'd done his homework, knew plenty about the vehicle and was prepared when he walked into the showroom.

It took him 15 minutes to find a salesperson who'd even talk to him. And when they eventually found a vehicle to take for a test drive, the salesperson knew absolutely nothing about it. Nothing.

Disgusted, my friend left the dealership vowing never to return.

He ended up buying a car he hadn't even considered because the salesperson he dealt with at the other dealership was outstanding. Of the six dealerships he'd visited, only one salesperson had even bothered to call him back with the answers to his questions. Guess who got the deal?

The Japanese have a very interesting phrase for customer service: "O Kyaku San." It means, "Honoured visitor in one's house."

I like that.

Have you ever noticed when you call someone at the office during the day, he usually answers the phone with an unseemly bark such as: "Lee here!"

It's almost as if they're saying, "What the heck do you want? I'm a busy and important person and you're not."

Call them at home at night and it's an oh-so-smooth, "Hello. Mr. Personality here. Oh, wrong number? Would you like to talk anyway?"

Ultimately, customer service is nothing more than treating customers as friends and I suppose treating friends as customers. Jack Harrison says the natural evolution goes something like this: Suspect, Prospect, Customer, Friend.

More than anything, customer service is an attitude of gratitude, it is an expression of appreciation. It is the highest honour to which you can aspire.

Chapter 1

Just "D.O. I.T." Checklist

Recommendations:

❏ 1. Smile and make eye contact. Say "please and thank you." Be a model for everyone.

❏ 2. Treat every customer as a friend. Better still as an "honoured visitor."

❏ 3. Don't underestimate the importance of your "telephone voice." Speak softly, as if you were at home.

*W*HO IS YOUR CUSTOMER, REALLY?

*"First we will be best
and then we will be first."*
– Grant Tinker

*I*t is nine o'clock on Monday morning. Do you know who your customer is?

Well if you said, "Everybody," you are probably on the right track. That may not be a bad approach, because anyone may be your customer today, or tomorrow, or sometime in the future.

If you don't deal directly with the people who utilize your organization's services or buy your company's products, perhaps you'd say your boss is your customer. One lady in a seminar got up and said, "My boss is really my only customer. Everything I do in the company, I do for him."

That may be true for you, too. It works the other way as well. Your staff might be your customers.

We just don't look at our co-workers as customers.

How about your suppliers? Does the way you treat them have anything to do with how well they treat you? As a matter of fact, there is a trend in the 90s to have our vendors or suppliers as partners, because of what a difference the results can make for an organization.

There are really two types of customers: external and internal.

The external is the most obvious. With a professional or business association, it's the member. For the government employee, it's the taxpayer. And in retail, it's the person buying your product. Simple.

But few of us consider the internal customer.

I always ask my audience if they consider themselves internal customers. Invariably, only a few brave souls will put up their hands. We just don't look at our co-workers as customers.

Think about it for a minute.

Does somebody write you a cheque every couple of weeks? Does somebody keep the place clean? Are there other people in the company who provide services to you? If you work in manufacturing, don't you depend on the next person in the production line?

You bet you do!

Yet perhaps you've never considered yourself a customer within your own organization before. You should. Because we are all internal customers. I believe in the 90s, the internal customer is just as important to us as the external one.

I was delivering a seminar at a hospital in Long Beach, California, and there was a lady there from admitting who had a real attitude problem.

Now I don't know about you, but from my experience I've come to wonder if it's a requirement to have an attitude problem if you work in admitting at a hospital.

In any case I pulled her aside and I said to her, "Listen, what's the problem here?"

She said, "Mr. Lee, if our customers are treated like a 10 out of 10, then we are treated like a two out of 10."

Guess how she was treating her patients?

Right. A two out of 10. Or worse.

What's that old saying about "What goes around comes around"?

It must be a pretty exceptional human being who will care for their customers when they, themselves, are being treated poorly, ordered around, or being treated without respect by the boss. Most employees treat customers better than they're treated by their bosses. Sad but true.

If the 1990s was the decade when we woke up to the importance of customer service, then the 21st Century should be the era when we recognize that treating our internal customers takes precedence over how we deal with our external customers.

It really is the beginning of everything we do.

Looking inside your organization is important but it's also crucial to look outside at the bigger picture.

Who is your customer? I was speaking at a city government seminar, and a storm and sewer manager said, "My customer is anyone who flushes a toilet." Big market!

Either a person is a customer now or
he is going to be sometime in the future.

Who is your customer? A realtor in Fort McMurray, Alberta, said, "Any live, warm body." Now there's a positive thinker and a positive attitude! I like that.

Either a person is a customer now or he is going to be sometime in the future. And that is a healthy way to look at it if you want your company, your government department, your non-profit organization, or your own career to grow and prosper in the decade ahead.

Chapter 2

Just " D.O. I.T." Checklist

Recommendations:

❏ 1. Treat anyone you provide a service to as your customer, including your boss and co-workers.

❏ 2. Make a list of your various types of customers and ask them "What can I do to serve you better?"

❏ 3. Serve others the way you'd like to be served.

*W*HY IS CUSTOMER SERVICE IMPORTANT?

"The average company loses 50 percent
of its customers every five years."
– The Loyalty Effect

*C*ar shopping can drive you batty.
Is there a difference between a Honda and a Yugo? About 15 grand, right? To the uninitiated, the Yugo might be the best buy, but the real difference is value. The Yugo has probably got the poorest resale performance of any car sold in North America today.

Is there a difference between a cheap suit and a good suit? You bet. I no longer look at what I have to pay for a suit. I've found that any suit worth less than $800 just doesn't stand up. I look at how many uses I will get out of it, amortized with my dry-cleaning bills.

It's called value.

People buy value, not price.

One truly great salesperson who also happens to be one of the most exceptional motivators of our time, Zig Ziglar, said: Value = Quality + Service – Price.

Why is customer service important? Because it adds value. That is exactly what people want.

Statistics say that a happy, satisfied customer will tell five people. An unhappy, unsatisfied customer will tell 10 people. An unhappy, unsatisfied professional speaker such as I, will tell 40,000 people!

I used to belong to an organization called the Jaycees and their motto was, "Service to humanity is the best work of life."

I really believe that.

I know what you're saying. You're saying, "Brian, you don't know what my job is. You don't know how hard I work."

Let's be honest. In the absence of being able to provide service to another human being, one on one, the best way you can, in a way that satisfies them – level with me here, now – can there really be any job satisfaction for you?

Ultimately, what is the one thing – the only thing – that can give you an advantage today? Customer Satisfaction, Customer Satisfaction, Customer Satisfaction.

People who believe that by giving only adequate service they're just ripping off their company are wrong. They're ripping themselves off as well. Can you imagine how endlessly long their working day must be?

Besides giving personal satisfaction, satisfying a customer doesn't hurt repeat business, either.

Statistics say that a happy, satisfied customer will tell five people. An unhappy, unsatisfied customer will tell 10 people. An unhappy, unsatisfied professional speaker will tell 40,000 people!

It will also help you get referrals; it is three times easier to close a sale with a referred lead than with a cold one.

Besides that, customer service will do wonders for the credibility of your organization. In a world where only about 80 percent of the agreements made in business are kept, credibility is so important. If you've got it, you're one up on your competitors.

Think about it. What have you got today that gives you a competitive advantage? Everybody has access to the same products, everybody buys at relatively the same price, everybody has access to the same technology and the same pool of labour from which to hire.

If you focus on service first, everything else has a way of falling into place.

Service, more than anything, is what's causing the customer revolution we're seeing in North America in the new millennium.

Customer service can also change your customer's perception of you. We spend a lot of money creating perception. It's called advertising. It costs five times as much to go out and find a new customer than it does to keep an existing one happy.

I used to work for a furniture store and before I started work there, it was an unequivocal disaster in terms of customer service. If people wanted their money back, they practically had to picket the place. Occasionally they did!

Ultimately, what is the one thing – the only thing
that can give you an advantage today?
Customer Satisfaction, Customer Satisfaction, Customer Satisfaction.

We spent a lot of time improving.

We also had to spend an average of seven percent of our gross income on advertising versus some of our competitors who were spending only three percent. You don't have to be a rocket scientist to know that spending four percent extra bribing your customers just to keep coming back is four percent out of your pocket.

That's right. From the bottom line. It's called lower profits.

Service. Customers are willing to pay for it.

Once you've got them, you'll have less trouble keeping them. Customer satisfaction creates loyalty. Not only will they be loyal to you, they will also be out selling for you all the time.

How many of you have walked into a car dealership and within the first 60 seconds you can tell the only thing the car salesperson wants to do is get his hand in your pocket?

Wouldn't you rather do business with a car sales representative "consultant" who wouldn't sell you anything you didn't need? Sure you would. That's why companies such as Saturn and dealerships of various types all over North America are evolving to one-price car shopping. People are tired of experiencing adversarial relationships during the purchase of a new vehicle.

I believe the only way you can make a profit today is by providing outstanding, exceptional, superb, customer satisfaction.

*If you focus on service first everything
else has a way of falling into place.*

If money is your only focus, I would suggest to you that it's almost impossible in today's economy to post a profit. Focus on service and the profit will come because satisfying your customers will pay you back many, many times over.

The statistics on this are overwhelming. You can expect quality service to do many things:

◆ increase prices by an average of nine percent;

◆ increase profit by an average of 11 percent;

◆ improve sales growth by an average of four percent; and

◆ increase job satisfaction and reduce staff turnover.

Interestingly, the highest return on investment is earned by industries with the highest training per employee per year. The rule of thumb is a simple one: Invest $1, get $10 back.

Like anything in life, to make it work you need to set goals. Your goals for customer service should read something like this:

◆ increase customer satisfaction by 10 percent;

◆ reduce customer complaints by 400 percent;

◆ improve customer retention by five percent;

◆ increase average sales per purchase by 3.25 percent;

*If you're going to be committed to good service,
do it for yourself, not for anybody else.*

◆ Reduce advertising expenses by half a percent;

◆ Increase employee suggestions by 600 percent;

◆ Decrease staff turnover by 20-35 percent;

◆ Reduce operating and administrative costs by 12 percent; and

◆ Enhance bottom line by a minimum of 3.5 percent.

Set those goals and customer service will pay, and pay, and pay.

I was in Toronto for a scheduled television appearance on "Canada AM." As I was checking into my hotel the night before, the front desk clerk noticed my address.

"Oh, Mr. Lee," she said excitedly, "I used to live two blocks from your office in Calgary."

I said, "Really? Why on earth would you move to Toronto?"

She told me that she had worked at a particular sister hotel in Calgary and asked me if I'd ever done business there.

I replied, somewhat indignantly, saying, "I would NEVER do business there."

This was supposed to be a four-star hotel. However, in reality, it provided two-star service, if that. She had moved to Toronto so she could work at a place that was committed to customer service excellence.

If you're going to be committed to good service, do it for yourself – not for anybody else.

17

Chapter 3

Just "D.O. I.T." Checklist

Recommendations:

❑ 1. For a three-month period, calculate the cost of acquiring new customers. Let everybody know.

❑ 2. The fastest way to improve your job/career satisfaction is to improve your customer satisfaction.

❑ 3. Act as if you were a "consultant" to your customer. Don't "suggest" ~ "recommend."

❑ 4. Work with your team to set specific; measurable goals for customer satisfaction. Share them with everyone.

$\mathcal{W}$HAT DO WE EXPECT AS CUSTOMERS?

SECRET #1
"Just meet your customer's
expectations and you'll be a STAR!"

$\mathcal{W}$hat's the most successful franchise in the world?
Of course, it's McDonald's. Not a tough question. We all eat there and the secret of their phenomenal success worldwide is their consistency.

I have eaten hamburgers at McDonald's in Canada, the United States, Hong Kong, Sydney, Australia, and Sydney, Nova Scotia. They are pretty much the same all over the world. The price varies greatly, but they taste the same wherever you go.

Taste is not their greatest feature. It's the consistency that counts.

Everywhere I speak, I ask my audiences the same thing: Tell me what you expect as a customer. Wherever I go, the list is basically the same. It usually reads something like this.

1 Empathy

We want to deal with people who care about our wants, our needs and our desires. Not sympathy; empathy for ourselves and the situation we're in.

My friend Jack was home with his two kids on a cold winter night when the furnace gave out.

He called for service and was treated rather rudely on the telephone. The serviceman showed up two hours later and his face-to-face demeanour was every bit as horrible as his phone manner. His grooming habits were worse. As the serviceman was leaving, my friend asked for the name of the president of the company.

"Is something wrong?" the employee asked, suddenly turning into Mr. Nice. When his shortcomings were aired, the furnace man immediately launched into a litany of excuses. He even said others in his organization were worse!

On a cold night when the heat isn't on, the last thing the customer needs to hear is what's bugging you. The customer wants and deserves empathy.

"When people want quality, they are willing to pay for it.
And when they want crap, they want it cheap."
– Tom Peters

---

2 Quality

The Profit Improvement

Management Survey says on average, we, as customers, will pay nine percent more for better quality. Tom Peters, author, speaker and a man who I admire very much says, "When people want quality, they are willing to pay for it. And when they want crap, they want it cheap."

3 Honesty

Like they used to say in that old TV series, Dragnet, "Just the facts ma'am."

4 Friendly

We don't want to deal with grumpy people. I understand you have problems but would you please look after me first before you tell me all your troubles. Half the people don't care and the other half think you deserve it.

5 Smile

Smile. It improves face value.

Have you ever walked into the office and said "Good morning" to someone and they say "Good morning" and you say "How are you?" and they say "Fine" and you say "Tell your face."

Smile. It improves face value.

6 Thank You

In some of the better hotels in Japan they pay people just to say "Goodbye" and "Thank you" as you go out the front door. They just stand there and thank you as you leave. It works so well they're now doing it at the Westin Hotel in Chicago.

7 Professionalism

If you can't be enthusiastic or friendly, at least be professional about your business.

8 Product knowledge

I live in hotels. Inevitably, when I go up in the elevator with the bellman, I ask, "What time does the coffee shop open in the morning?" Nine times out of 10 they'll say, "I don't know."

Then I'll ask them, "What time does the steam room close at night?" They say, "I don't know." So I say, "What hotel do you work for?" I assume they don't know.

Room service is no better. Nine out of every 10 times you ask them what the soup of the day is, they say they don't know. Then they bang the phone down on the counter and leave your ear ringing.

I'm wondering if they're not allowed to know?

Does anyone you know work in a shopping centre? Take a good look at them. They're different. Because they never, ever have to go to the bathroom. Ask any employee in a shopping centre where the bathroom is and they don't know.

When I work with shopping centres, the first thing I tell them is take your new employees on a three-hour tour of the place. It is essential.

21

9 Flexibility and Personalized Service

We want the organization to adapt to us. We don't want to have to adapt to the organization.

I was at a shopping mall awhile ago and I was standing in a line at one of those frozen yogurt places. The people in front of me had placed their orders so I told the person behind the counter what I wanted.

"You'll have to stand over there to place your order," she said, pointing to a "Place Order Here" sign. "But I already ordered and I'm standing here. What difference does it make?" I asked.

"Well if you don't stand in the right place, how will I know who's next?"

Perhaps she hadn't thought of looking up between scoops.

Now this wasn't her fault. Don't misunderstand. This loyal 17-year-old employee had been told those were the rules and she was doing her sunday best to follow them.

As customers, however, we'd appreciate a little flexibility.

My friend Doug was in a book store recently.

The fellow in front of him at the checkout counter had bought a stack of books and requested a handwritten receipt. He needed it for the boss.

Well the clerk was obviously miffed. She didn't say she was miffed but sometimes it's not that difficult to tell.

She spent more time trying to tell the guy her automatic receipt from the till would be good enough, than it would have taken to give him what he'd asked for.

Meanwhile, she left him angry and a lineup of customers frustrated with the wait.

Do it right the first time.

When my friend asked her why she hadn't just given him what he'd asked for instead of wasting time arguing about it, she shoved his bag of magazines across the counter and barked, "I didn't know we were arguing."

Be flexible. That's what customers want.

10 Efficiency

Do it right the first time.

11 Timeliness

When you go into a restaurant, you don't want to have to beg the waitress, "Please, please, please, can I have another cup of coffee?"

You don't want to be told, as I was told recently, "I'm sorry Mr. Lee, you'll have to go. The next reservation is here."

12 Value

Remember the formula. Value = Quality + Service − Price.

13 Safety

When I'm on an airplane, I don't want to hear that there's a one percent risk factor because I travel a hundred times a year.

14 Organization

Get organized. Your internal problems are of no interest to your customer.

15 Courtesy

I don't know who said it, but whoever said it was right: "Common courtesy is so uncommon." Rodney Dangerfield always says, "I don't get no respect." What makes Rodney Dangerfield think he's so different from anybody else?

16 Variety

We want selection that is appropriate. I once met a woman named Myrtle who was 76. She told me that in the 76 years she had lived in Sault Ste. Marie, she had never been able to get a shoe that was a 9$^{1}/_{2}$ B. She said if any shoes came into the store that happened to be the right size for her, the employees always bought them first.

17 Motivation

Don't you love it when you go into a store and a clerk says, "Can I help you?" in a tone that tells you they'd really rather not. When someone says, "Can I help you?" to me, I always ask if I'm in some kind of trouble.

All it takes is a little creativity. How about, "Welcome," or, "Good to see you"? How about, "How the heck are you?" or, if they are Baptists, "How in Heaven's name are you?"

I once went into a million and a half dollar restaurant in Sacramento – a million and a half bucks! The receptionist said in a rather snotty way, "Just one?" Then I went back with my friend and she says, "Just two?"

Exactly how many did we need? Obviously, I wasn't the only one who felt that way about the place or they might still be operating today.

18 Recognition

We want to be thanked. We want to be recognized. The number one reason people go to expensive restaurants is not for the food. It's for the recognition.

How about, "Mr. Lee, your table is ready. Will that be a Big Mac or a Quarter Pounder?"

The number one reason people go to expensive restaurants is not for the food. It's for the recognition.

My friend Tim was at a golf resort in Hawaii and the people working at the golf course were largely indifferent. Like so many places, a $100 green fee was no guarantee of good service.

There was one exception.

One jovial local, whose duty was to load the golf carts and clean clubs, a task most would consider menial, was always kibitzing with the customers. He remembered everyone's name.

He made sure he found out who wanted to play with whom and he quickly learned the hierarchy of the group. The tourists were suitably impressed and at week's end, the cart jockey got a tip of several hundred dollars. His fellow employees got nothing.

Believe it. Recognition counts.

19 Listened to

We want to be really listened to and not in a condescending way.

20 Understood

Not patronized.

21 Patience

As customers, we don't know everything you know about your business, so lighten up.

22 Uninterrupted

I was checking out of a hotel not too long ago. I was running late and the taxi was sitting outside waiting for me.

I had asked the hotel to make up my bill in advance but, unfortunately, they hadn't. When I got to the front desk, the guy took not one, not two, not three, but four phone calls as I stood there looking nervously at my watch.

With the taxi waiting and my departure time looming, he was about to take a fifth call when I barked, "Don't touch that phone!"

What a person is saying when they won't look at you:
"I don't trust you. I don't want to deal with you."

When you are dealing with someone, priority should be given to the person who is in front of you, with two exceptions: you are a receptionist or you work for the fire department.

23 Eye contact

What is a person saying when they won't look at you? "I don't want to talk to you. I don't trust you. I don't want to deal with you."

In our increasingly multicultural society, be aware of cultural differences. Some people don't believe in the kind of eye contact North Americans appreciate.

24 Loyalty

We want to be remembered and considered.

25 Appearance

Is it how much you spend on appearance? No. It's what you do with what you've got.

26 Cleanliness

If you're in a restaurant and you go into the bathroom, what do you think of the place if there is no toilet paper and no soap? Yuck! I wonder what the kitchen looks like?

John Munro was fed up with dirty bathrooms. He happens to be in the Greyhound bus business and there are 900 terminals in Canada where it had become pretty dicey to answer a nature call.

He was getting sick of hearing about how awful the bathrooms were and when he gave his wife a pass to take the bus to Vancouver, even she refused to use the ladies room.

John sent out a memo.

Memo.

From: *John Munro*

To: *Terminal Operators*

Subject: *Terminal Bathrooms*

"I'm going to be having dinner once a month from now on in one of our terminal bathrooms, with the regional vice-president and the terminal manager and I'm not going to say where and I'm not going to say when."

My compliments to John Munro for making a difference. By the way, this was no idle threat. His phone number is in every bathroom run by Greyhound in Canada. I encourage all of you to check out his facilities!

While the airline industry is getting better in this regard, they haven't caught on as quickly as you might like. Have you ever been on an airplane and you drop the tray table to find it's filthy? If that's how they maintain the cabin, how, one might ask, are they looking after maintenance of the engines? I don't want to know.

Add all of this up and what do you get?

No, not service. The answer is satisfaction. Six Star Customer Satisfaction.

You would probably agree this is what you want as a customer.

♦ Do you get it very often?

♦ Are you tired of not getting it?

♦ Will you stand up and say you're angry and you're not going to take it anymore?

♦ What would be the value if everyone in your organization knew this, understood it, and acted on it? Could you put a price on it?

♦ What is the point of making the list of expectations? What's the value in understanding this concept and putting it into practice?

The point (and subsequently the value) is anybody who takes the time to meet their customers' expectations will be one up on everyone else. As I said before, your competitors have access to the same services, the same capital and labour pool as you and only Total Customer Satisfaction will set you apart.

If that's what we expect, maybe, just maybe, that's what we ought to give.

You cannot have it both ways. You can't give only average service and expect good service in return because life doesn't work that way. You get out of any job, relationship, business or organization only what you put into it.

Let people know when you're getting bad service because you're not doing anybody any favours by letting them get away with it. What goes around comes around.

Can you name three places in the community where you live that consistently meet your expectations?

1._____

2._____

3._____

Probably not.

Only a handful of people can come up with even one, and that generally makes people just a little uncomfortable.

More importantly, look in the mirror. Would your organization make the list?

In a world of mediocrity, just meet your customer's expectations and people will beat a path to your door.

There is a whole school of thought out there that says exceed your customer's expectations and you'll do well. That's nice.

Just for a start, try this.

1. We are either part of the solution or we are part of the problem. It's a cliché but there is wisdom in clichés. That's why they are clichés.

2. In a world of mediocrity, just meet your customer's expectations and people will beat a path to your door. We simply are not used to it.

3. Service excellence is a passion for the intangibles. It's not the product you sell. Oh no. It's how people feel about the product when you give it to them that counts. Service can be good, but the real challenge is satisfaction; the real challenge is meeting needs and expectations.

4. "Everybody's gotta serve somebody." I don't know if Bob Dylan had that in mind but it's true. The problem is a mentality out there that says working in customer service is being subservient to someone else. It's something you do until you can get a good job.

The interesting thing is these expectations are the same for everybody. I've conducted this customer "expectation" exercise all over the world with more than a quarter of a million people and the list doesn't change.

It's not difficult to do this exercise because we're all customers. Just meet expectations, consistently, period, and your business and your reputation will grow, regardless of what's happening in the economy.

Of course, you might not be in the business of giving service, but you are, as we all are, in the business of being customers.

I had a lady in a seminar come up to me once and say, "Brian, I came here today to learn how to be a better customer."

Huh? Say what?

You know, the more I thought about it the more I realized she was right. The clearer you are about how to give good service, the more you'll understand about how to get it and what to expect.

I'll tell you what. I get great service . . . everywhere I go, because I expect it.

I was in a hotel that has a policy, like many hotels do, that you have to get your dry-cleaning in by 9 a.m. and it would be out by 6 p.m.

Except my life doesn't work that way.

I needed my suit by three so I could be at the hall early that night. I phoned the front desk and asked if there was a dry-cleaner nearby that could clean my suit in an hour.

They were happy to do it. They found one so I asked them to find a bellman to take the suit over for me.

"I'm not sure we can do that," said the clerk.

"Well, just call the duty manager and ask," I said.

A few minutes later, the bellman knocked at my door and I got my suit dry-cleaned.

The clearer you are about what you expect, the sooner you'll start getting it. The sooner you start giving it, the sooner you'll start getting it back.

I deliver management seminars, and traditionally we've thought of a business as a pyramid with managers on the top and customers at the bottom. That's probably what they told you in college.

Well, the new winners today realize that the customer is THE most important person in the organization and the pyramid has been inverted. The role of managers is to support the real heroes of the organization, the people who serve the customers.

In high school I worked at Safeway. It was kind of neat when I got to present a seminar on customer service for the Safeway stores in the state of Texas. I asked all of these managers in the room how much a typical customer would spend in a week. The answer was about $100. Multiply that by 52 weeks a year if you will.

I asked them how many customers an average cashier will deal with in a month. "About a thousand," they replied.

Get out your calculator. That means one cashier, good, bad or indifferent, can impact $5 million worth of business in a year.

I went out into the audience and there, in the front row, was the president. I asked him, "Level with me. How much do you, personally, have to do with the success of that $5 million worth of business?"

He was honest.

"Nothing," he confessed.

When was the last time a president of a grocery store chain ever looked after a customer? Ditto for the managers. Most of them wouldn't know how to operate a till if their lives depended on it.

Do you know why bank managers don't work as tellers anymore? Because they don't know how to work the computers. They don't. It is the cashiers and the tellers of this world who make a difference.

I asked the store managers in Texas how long they keep an average customer? They said, "Ten years if we're lucky."

. . . the most expensive liability any organization has is a poorly trained employee.

And that, folks, is $50 million worth of business One cashier, good, bad, or indifferent.

I've reached the conclusion that the most expensive liability any organization has is a poorly trained employee. There are no savings whatsoever in hiring cheap labour and not training them. An employee is not a cost to be controlled or contained but an asset to be empowered and developed.

As Jethro Bodine on the Beverley Hillbillies used to say, "I'll do the ciphering, Granny." Work out the mathematics of it because training does pay off. So does going that little extra step.

An employee is not a cost to be controlled or contained but an asset to be empowered and trained.

Like the time I was out jogging and I pulled into a 7-11 to buy some aspirin and some batteries for my Walkman.

When I went to pay for the stuff the guy behind the counter asked me if I'd like a glass of water.

"Water? Why would I want water?" I said, not thinking as clearly as he was.

"Well, you look a little rough," he said sheepishly, "and you bought some aspirins so I thought you might want . . ."

The man has a great future!

I was checking into a Stouffer's Hotel in Florida one time and there was a very long lineup. I hear it happens often but they have a way of dealing with it. While you're waiting in line, they bring you a glass of champagne.

Perfect.

I could have waited in line for hours.

In Dallas, there is a Cadillac dealership owned by a man named Carl Sewell. Now this isn't just any Cadillac dealership. Sewell Village Cadillac is the most successful Cadillac dealership in Texas.

When you get your car serviced what are the three things that usually go wrong?

Well, often the final bill bears no resemblance to the estimate. Usually, the car isn't ready when you've been promised it. You might have to take the car back again and again and again to correct the same problem.

At Sewell Village Cadillac in Dallas, they have a very clear policy and everybody knows it.

If the final bill is more than the estimate – it's free.

If the car is not ready when we say it will be ready – it's free.

If you have to bring the car back for the same repair twice – it's free.

Now of course they are very careful – perhaps even overly generous in their estimates – but it works. The results speak for themselves.

. . . service excellence is a passion, not for the tangibles,
but for the intangibles.

Meet your customer's expectations and by definition you will exceed your customer's expectations. Even better – lead your customer's expectations. Find out what they want next and you will be a service superstar.

I've come to the conclusion that service excellence is a passion not for the tangibles, but for the intangibles.

Michael LeBoeuf wrote a book called *How to Win Customers and Keep Them For Life*, and this is what he said:

> "Don't sell me clothes. Sell me a sharp appearance, style and attractiveness.

31

Don't sell me insurance. Sell me peace of mind and a great future for my family and me.

Don't sell me a house. Sell me comfort, contentment, a good investment and pride of ownership.

Don't sell me books. Sell me pleasant hours and the profits of knowledge.

Don't sell me toys. Sell my children happy moments.

Don't sell me a computer. Sell me the pleasures and profits of the miracles of modern technology.

Don't sell me tires. Sell me freedom from worry and low-cost per mile.

Don't sell me airline tickets. Sell me a fast, safe, on-time arrival at my destination feeling like a million dollars.

Don't sell me things. Sell me ideals, feelings, self-respect, home, life and happiness.

Please don't sell me things."

There really are only two things people buy: feelings and solutions to problems.

Don't take my word for it. Go back to your list. Where on that list is there anything tangible? Okay, there are a couple of things, but out of two dozen, most are intangibles; the little things.

What do most managers manage? They manage the tangibles. Who will compete and succeed and prosper in the 90s? I think you know the answer.

There is a new world out there and we'd better adapt.

Chapter 4

Just "D.O. I.T." Checklist

Recommendations:

❏ 1. Make a list of all of your customer's expectations. Prioritize the top six and do whatever it takes to meet them.

❏ 2. Be sincere! (Whether you mean it or not.)

❏ 3. It's OK to be friendly. At a minimum, be professional.

❏ 4. Get to know where everything is and what everyone does. Your customers expect it.

❏ 5. Don't make your customers adapt to you. Adapt to them.

❏ 6. Smile. It's contagious (except when removing stitches).

❏ 7. Make an effort to remember and recognize your customers.

❏ 8. Practice good grooming habits. Toothbrush and mouthwash are tools of your trade.

❏ 9. Anticipate.

❏ 10. Focus on the intangibles.

*T*HE SIX STAR™ PHILOSOPHY

"It's not your Aptitude
but your Attitude that
determines your Altitude"
— Napoleon Hill

*Y*ou probably earned your first gold star in grade school. We thought it was a big deal back then and we still put a lot of stock in the stars.

Do you know what they really mean when it comes to service? You know, four-star restaurants, five-star hotels and the like?

Every year the latest star ratings from Mobil and the American and Canadian Automobile Associations are published. Every state and province seems to have their own rating list as well.

The only thing consistent between them is that the most a Bed & Breakfast can be awarded is two stars. I know many people who've stayed in B&Bs and have had a wonderful experience, perhaps the best stay they've ever had.

I stayed at a place in Fredericton, New Brunswick, called the Carriage House. The service was so exceptional that I had the privilege of jogging with Jake the Irish Setter (or should I say Jake took me out for a "run").

Our philosophy, "Six Star Customer Satisfaction," is based on the "six values of lifetime loyalty."

THE SIX VALUES OF LIFETIME LOYALTY:

1 Your Customer

He or she is the star of the business, not you. Your success is based on your ability to understand your customer's expectations and meet them.

2 Communication

The way you communicate with your customers determines your relationship with them.

3 Systems

The most successful franchise in the world is McDonalds. Their genius is their consistency.

4 Attitude

Attitude is everything. As Napoleon Hill once said, "It's not your aptitude but your attitude that determines your altitude."

---

*The way you treat your people will determine
how your people treat your customers.*

---

5 People

The way you treat your people will determine how your people treat your customers.

6 Quality product and service

I don't know what you make or sell, but I do know about the concept of excellence. The term is so overused it has become trite. Excellence, however, is really continuous improvement.

---

*... we really rate our stay on subjective criteria: how we were
welcomed at the front desk, the friendliness of the service or the
temperature of the Jacuzzi – the intangibles.*

I bet you've been to a four-star restaurant that had bad service. In fact, the rating of a hotel or restaurant has very little, if anything, to do with how you and I, as customers, feel about its service.

In other words, hotels and restaurants are rated on tangibles. Does the hotel have a pool? A coffee shop? An exercise facility?

The way you and I really rate a hotel isn't based on any of these things. It's based almost entirely on how we feel. Sure, we'd like those other things if we've paid for them. But we really rate our stay on more subjective criteria, how we were welcomed at the front desk, the friendliness of the service or the temperature of the Jacuzzi – the intangibles.

If you're into the outdoors or at least into looking like you're into the outdoors, then you've probably heard of a company called L.L. Bean, a $550 million-a-year mail order business based in Freeport, Maine, population 5,863. They are really committed to service.

As a matter of fact, I read a story a little while ago about a farmer who bought a pair of boots from L.L. Bean about 20 years ago. After 20 years the boots were looking pretty shabby. (No doubt!) In fact, they were worn out.

But this farmer figured he didn't get enough trips to the barn and back out of these boots so he contacted L.L. Bean and took them back for a full refund!

L.L. Bean does this all the time. Will they get ripped off with this kind of a policy? Of course, they will.

Their motto, and I've made this a motto of my company too, is outstanding.

"The customer is the most important person to this office, in person or by mail.

A customer is not dependent on us; we are dependent on them.

A customer is not an interruption of our work; they are the purpose of it.

We are not doing a favor by serving them; they are doing us a favor by giving us the opportunity to do so.

A customer is not someone to argue or match wits with. Nobody ever won an argument with a customer.

A customer is a person who brings us their wants. It is our job to handle them so that it is profitable to them and to ourselves."

Maybe, just maybe, this should be a motto for us all.

Chapter 5

Just "D.O. I.T." Checklist

Recommendations:

❏ 1. Make a commitment to consistently deliver the "Six Star" values of lifetime customer loyalty.

❏ 2. Ask yourself every day before you start work, "If attitude were contagious, would I want anyone to catch mine?"

❏ 3. Consider the customer in everything that you do.

COMMUNICATION

SECRET #2 "Customers judge you by:
The way you look, what you say,
how you say it, what you do,
how you do it."
— DALE CARNEGIE

*C*an you guess what percentage of communication is words only? Go ahead. Guess. Is it five? Ten? Twenty? Fifty?

None of the above. The correct answer is . . . seven percent.

Skeptical?

Think about it. Other than the spoken word, how do human beings communicate? (I don't mean by using fax machines!)

1 Hand gestures and body language

We use an average of 12,000 words in our day-to-day vocabulary. There are over 600,000 meanings that can be conveyed with hand gestures and body language . . . just watch:

– Italians speaking with their hands;

– the John Wayne "walk."

2 Eye contact . . . "the window to the soul"

Have you ever tried to kiss someone without first establishing eye contact?

Get into some creative grunting if you must. "Yes. I see.
Uh huh. Is that right?" Listen as if you plan to report or
to teach what it is you're listening to.

We've all worked for an employer who claimed the door was always open. But every time you went in, he or she would continue working, and look away while you spoke. It doesn't work. Give each person your undivided attention.

3 Listening

Get into some creative grunting if you must, especially on the phone. "Yes. I see. Uh huh. Is that right?" Listen as if you plan to report or to teach what it is you're listening to.

4 Restating

Repeat what was said just to make sure you got it right. Have you ever wasted an hour, perhaps a day, doing a project that wasn't the right project, just because you didn't restate what you were told?

5 Beware of emotional deaf spots

If you just got a divorce, how enthused were you the next day about talking marriage? When I was in politics, my emotional deaf spot came when my opponents were arguing against me. When should I have been listening? We tend to tune out those who complain.

6 Attitude is everything

What can I say . . .

7 Appearance

Above all, be "appropriate" for your customers.

8 Personal space

The most powerful form of personal communication is touch. Whoever does the touching has the power. When I was in politics, I used to regularly visit senior citizens residences. I didn't go to talk politics, though.

I went there to hug. The Mental Health Association says we need seven hugs a day, just for maintenance, seven more for growth.

> *. . . people will judge you in the first seven seconds*
> *from a menu of over 200 attributes.*

9 Grooming and hygiene

We had a very awkward situation in our office awhile back with a lady who wore leather pants that smelled. We debated for three months over who was going to tell her. She needed some feedback.

10 Enthusiasm

We all love it as long as it's not too early in the morning.

11 Smile

Don't underestimate what a smile is worth.

THE VALUE OF A SMILE

> *It costs nothing, but creates much.*
>
> *It enriches those who receive, without impoverishing those who give.*
>
> *It happens in a flash and the memory of it sometimes lasts forever.*
>
> *None are so rich that they can get along without it and none are so poor but are richer for its benefits.*
>
> *It creates happiness in the home, fosters good will in a business and is the countersign of friends.*
>
> *It is rest to the weary, daylight to the discouraged, sunshine to the sad and nature's best antidote for trouble.*
>
> *Yet it cannot be bought, begged, borrowed, or stolen for it is something that is no earthly good to anybody till it is given away!*
>
> *And if it ever happens that some of our people should be too tired to give you a smile, may we ask you to leave one of yours?*
>
> *For nobody needs a smile so much as those who have none left to give.*
>
> *from Dale Carnegie – "How to Win Friends"*

41

A smile is powerful stuff, every business should display it prominently.

I met a guy in one of my seminars who told me his wife almost divorced him because he sleeps with a smile on his face and she doesn't know why!

Wanna have some fun in an elevator? Turn around and smile.

A smile improves face value.

Out of compassion for our environment alone we need to smile, because it costs three times as much energy to frown. So lighten up.

I'm proud of the fact that the most successful McDonald's in the world is in Moscow and it's run by a Canadian. He went over to Russia, hired 2,000 Muscovites and brought them over to North America to teach them how to smile. They went back and started smiling and it frightened the heck out of their fellow citizens. Of course, the only people who smiled in Moscow before the Golden Arches were KGB.

A smile mirrors how we feel. We smile when we feel good. Therefore a smile can impact how we feel.

Be careful. You can change how you feel just by smiling. As they say in the theatre, "Fake it until you make it." When I'm angry before a seminar, I go on stage smiling. I mean, who wants to listen to an angry speaker, right? Usually by the break I've forgotten what I was angry about. Do not tell the world your problems. They don't want to know. Half the people don't want to hear it and the other half think you deserve it anyway.

And never, ever, ever phone in sick when you're not. Ever done it?

When you phone in sick, how do you have to sound? Sick. How do you feel when you hang up? Sick. "Lucky I phoned in."

The subconscious can't tell the difference between imagination and a real experience. Therefore, what I suggest you do is phone in well. "Hi boss. It's a great day. I'm not coming in." Tell 'em Brian Lee said so!

You see, it's more than just what you say. It's how you say it. What you do while you say it. How people react to how you say it. In fact, people will judge you in the first seven seconds from a menu of over 200 attributes.

I wear a bow tie. It's my trademark. Yet how many of you would make a snap judgement the minute you met a guy in a bow tie? Is it Pee Wee Herman or Senator Paul Simon?

When your customer walks through the front door, do what you can to make certain the first impression is a good one. Because as this poem suggests, you tell on yourself.

YOU TELL ON YOURSELF

You tell on yourself by the friends you seek
by the very manner in which you speak
by the way you employ your leisure time
by the use you make of dollars and time.

You tell what you are by the things you wear
by the spirit in which your burdens bear
by the kind of things at which you laugh
by the records you play on your phonograph

You tell what you are by the way you walk
by the things of which you delight to talk
by the manner in which you bear defeat
by so simple a thing as how you eat

By the books you choose from a well-filled shelf
in these ways and more you tell on yourself
so there's really no particle of sense
in an effort to keep up false pretense
you tell on yourself.
                              Author unknown.

Chapter 6

Just "D.O. I.T." Checklist

Recommendations:

❏ 1. Be aware that customers "read you" non-verbally within the first seven seconds of contact.

❏ 2. Be certain you read your customers.

❏ 3. Watch out for emotional deaf spots – what your customers don't like about you.

$\mathcal{P}$ERCEPTION
= DECEPTION

SECRET #3
"What I believe doesn't count
What my customer perceives does."

$\mathcal{A}$ grocery store is a grocery store is a grocery store. Right? Everybody needs one. Every town has one.

We should all be so lucky to shop at a place like Stew Leonard's. Maybe you've never even heard of them, but Stew Leonard's is the most successful food store in the world. Bar none.

They sell $120 million+ worth of groceries every year in one store in Connecticut. They are the exception, selling 10 times the industry average per square foot even though they only stock 750 items instead of the 24,000 items most grocery stores carry.

I probably don't have to tell you that Stew Leonard's is obsessed with customer service.

They meet in focus groups with a handful of their customers every week. At that meeting, the store asks how they're doing, what the customers like and don't like and what Stew Leonard's can do better.

One particular incident in one of those meetings, featured in the PBS documentary "In Search of Excellence," illustrates perfectly what Stew Leonard's is all about.

At this particular meeting, a lady said, "I think you should sell fresh fish."

"Well, we do sell fresh fish," replied a somewhat perplexed management type.

"No, I want fresh fish," she said.

"But we do sell fresh fish," he protested.

"Well I think it ought to be fresh," she insisted.

"Rule No. 1: The customer is always right.
Rule No. 2: When the customer is wrong, see rule number one."
– Stew Leonard

"But it is," the manager stammered. "We buy it daily, wrap it, pack it, put it in the cooler and if it doesn't sell that day, we throw it away."

What does fresh fish look like? Of course, swimming would be really fresh. She was thinking about fish market fish: on ice, full head, staring you in the eye.

Now at Stew Leonard's they have two rules about customer service which they're so committed to, that the rules are carved into a 6,000-pound rock at the entrance to the store.

Rule No. 1: The customer is always right.

Rule No. 2: When the customer is wrong, see rule number one.

By the way, just for the record, is the customer always right?

No, of course not.

They've been known to lie, cheat, steal and have selective hearing. However, what most of us do is take the rules for the two percent who really are a pain in the neck and apply them to the other 98 percent who are good people. The customer may not always be right, but the customer IS the customer and they deserve the same service and respect that you do.

Meanwhile, back at Stew Leonard's, they continued to sell fish the way they always had and it continued to sell well – 15,000 pounds a week.

Across the aisle, in response to the insistent woman at the focus group, the new display of fresh fish was also selling, selling to the tune of 15,000 pounds a week.

Total fish sales had doubled.

Conclusion?

Perception = Deception.

And perception is all that matters.

Do you really know how your customers perceive you?

Only one in 26 customers will bother to complain.

I was delivering a seminar on the West Coast and there was a woman in the seminar who stood up and said, "I know exactly how our customers perceive us."

Okay, I thought to myself, maybe she's the exception. There were 59 of her coworkers present and I said to her, "Do you mind if I ask the audience?"

She said, "Go ahead."

So I asked the audience, "How many people here would agree that this department store consistently meets your expectations?"

Nine hands went up out of 200. Nine, in a packed house, not even her 51 coworkers agreed with her. They called an emergency meeting for the next day.

Now some of you are probably saying, "C'mon Brian. I talk to my customers every day."

Soooooo what!

When was the last time you had a bad meal in a restaurant and you actually contacted the manager and said you had a bad meal, told them you weren't happy with the way things were and said you were never coming back again?

We just don't do it.

As a matter of fact, only one in 26 customers will bother to complain. If you've got four or five written complaints, you've got a major perception problem on your hands.

. . . 68 percent, almost seven out of 10 customers, leave us because they think we don't care.

Why don't we complain?

Because it takes time, because we can't be bothered, because people get mad at us when we do and because we think management doesn't do anything about it. We just don't bother.

Let's take it a step farther. Let's look at why customers come and go.

◆ The statistics say one percent die.

(I shared this at a seminar in a hospital in Maine and a surgeon in the audience says, "Brian, that's kind of low isn't it?" I had an undertaker say, "Well Brian, all my customers are dead." We're talking average, here.)

◆ Five percent develop other friendships.

◆ Nine percent leave for competitive reasons.

◆ Fourteen percent are dissatisfied with the product.

◆ And here's the clincher: 68 percent, almost seven out of 10 customers, leave us because they think we don't care.

They don't stop to say their goodbyes. They simply do not come back. When was the last time you were dissatisfied and actually went by the place to stick your head in the door and say, "Take a good look at this kisser because you'll never see it again."

Stew Leonard takes a different approach.

"I don't mind the customer who complains," says the grocer extraordinaire. "It's the one who doesn't complain that worries me. The one who complains is like your best friend because they give you the opportunity to improve. The one who doesn't complain just doesn't come back."

My friend Leo was pricing computer software over the phone. When he called one place, the guy on the other end of the phone said, "I'm real busy. I'll call you back."

He took my friend's name and number and never called. This year, my friend will probably do a few thousand dollars worth of business with another store that took the time to give him what he needed.

Ask yourself this question: What motivates you to buy? What motivates all customers?

If there are only three things from this book you take with you and put into practice at your place of business, remember these three:

Number one, it doesn't matter how you deliver service. What matters is how your customers perceive the service you deliver.

Number two, the key to excellent service is to under-promise and over-deliver. I'd bet 99 percent of organizations do exactly the opposite. Everybody is over-promising and under-delivering. The end result can only be one thing: Disappointment.

Number three, what gets measured gets done. The things you pay attention to in your business, the things you measure, are the things that change.

Chapter 7

Just "D.O. I.T." Checklist

Recommendations:

❏ 1. Practice the two rules of Customer Satisfaction

Rule No. 1: The customer is always right

Rule No. 2: When the customer is wrong, see rule number one.

❏ 2. Be aware that we usually see ourselves differently than our customers do. It takes about 100 days to grow "blinders."

❏ 3. Make darn sure your customer doesn't leave you because of an attitude of indifference.

.

*W*HY DO CUSTOMERS COMPLAIN?

*"It takes extra gas
to become world class."*
— Brian Lee CSP

*H*otels-R-Us.

I spend an awful lot of time on the road and unfortunately, I have far too many tales to tell about hotels that didn't quite get it right.

I had been delivering a Six Star seminar and I had to fly that night to Ottawa. By the time I got there, got my luggage, rented a car and made it to the hotel, it was 12:30 in the morning. I had to wait for 10 minutes while the clerk argued with another customer and then another 20 minutes while he checked in 12 airline personnel who had arrived after I did.

At that point he told me he didn't have a room.

---

*I pointed across the hotel lobby and said to the clerk,
"You can just make up that couch right there. That'll do."*

Lovely.

I had made a "guaranteed reservation" and you know how that works. If I hadn't made it there that night, I'd have been charged for the room anyway. No ifs, ands or buts.

The clerk said I'd have to stay at another hotel.

I asked, "Why didn't you tell me that 25 minutes ago?"

"I was busy," he said.

"Well why did you check those airline people in ahead of me?" I inquired.

"Because they had a guaranteed reservation," he replied.

Good grief.

This happens to me far too often. I pointed across the hotel lobby and said to the clerk, "You can just make up that couch right there. That'll do."

"I'm sorry sir. We can't do that."

I said, "I'll tell you what. Does this hotel have cots? I have rented a meeting room here. You make me up a cot and I'll sleep in the meeting room."

Now he wasn't sure what to do.

The security guard, overhearing a conversation that was rapidly deteriorating, stepped in with an offer of help.

"I can do that for you Mr. Lee," he said.

At 2:30 in the morning, I slipped into my jogging suit and climbed into my cot for what was left of the night in the middle of half a hotel ballroom.

They woke me up at 3:30 a.m. and said, "Mr. Lee, we've found you a room."

I said, "I'm not moving. If you want me to move, then you move me."

They moved me.

When I woke up the next morning and went downstairs for a meeting with the client, the cot had been removed from the meeting room.

I said, "Who told you to take the cot out?"

"Well," they replied, "we thought you'd want it out."

"No," I smiled knowingly, "I want it back."

My seminar that morning was called "In Search of Excellence." I don't have to spell the rest out for you, do I?

I had a mini-seminar on customer service the next day with the hotel manager and his assistant. We talked about what *hadn't* happened the night before that should have happened.

WHY DO CUSTOMERS COMPLAIN?

1. "Because they didn't get what they were promised." I was promised a room and didn't get it.

2. "An employee was rude on the phone or in person." This employee was not only rude, he was indignant that I would be upset.

3. "A feeling of indifference." He didn't care that I waited 25 minutes for him to deal with my problem.

4. "A perception that no one was listening." It was no sweat off his back that I had to be up in a few hours to give a seminar.

5. "An employee projected a "can't do" or negative attitude." What does a can't do or negative attitude sound like? "It's policy."

On another occasion, I was staying in a hotel in New York and I called down to the front desk to ask them to send up a banquet chair so I could actually sit at my desk and do some work.

He said, "No, I can't sir, it's policy."

Right. On page 1342 of the hotel manual it says, "If a customer wants a banquet chair in the room, you can't give it to him because he will steal it along with the hotel towels."

You know as well as I do there wasn't any policy. He just didn't want to do it.

I said to him, "You have the general manager call me and tell me why you can't do it."

The chair was delivered a couple of minutes later.

Instead of saying "It's policy" explain the reason(s). If you really don't know, ask the boss. If the boss doesn't know, have them ask his boss. And if his boss doesn't know, then perhaps you have a "Sacred Cow."

What's a "Sacred Cow"?

It is something you do because you've always done it that way even if you don't know why you still do it.

When I was on city council in Calgary, I was asked to vote to rescind a bylaw that made it illegal to push a dead horse through the streets of the city. Now, personally, I think it would be easier to pull a dead horse, but what do I know?

You can see why they needed the bylaw back in 1910. Without it, there would have been horse heads everywhere. Gross. But in today's world, we didn't need the bylaw.

How many "Sacred Cow" horse bylaws do you have? Ask "Why?" and do something about it.

Customers want action and solutions, they want commitment, they want timely responses and they want individual, personalized attention. They also want value.

To the hotel's credit in Ottawa, they went out of their way to make up for their not-so-little faux pas.

They cancelled the bill, comped me the room and bought my dinner. So they should have. What they did was inexcusable.

They wrote me a letter to apologize and I went back and did business with them again.

NOTICE

I do not consider a sale complete until goods are worn out and the customer is still satisfied.

We will thank anyone to return goods that are not perfectly satisfactory.

Should the person reading this notice know of anyone who is not satisfied with our goods, I will consider it a favor to be notified.

Above all things, we wish to avoid having a dissatisfied customer.

Sign in L.L. Bean store, Freeport, Maine.

Chapter 8

Just "D.O. I.T." Checklist

Recommendations:

❏ 1. Never say "it's policy." Give the reason for the policy.

❏ 2. If you cannot find the reason for a policy, it's probably a "Sacred Cow." Change it. Besides, "Sacred Cows" make great steaks and that's all.

❏ 3. Make sure you communicate a "can do," not a "can't do" attitude.

MESS UP, FESS UP, DRESS UP

"Whoever hears a complaint becomes the customer's saint."
— Brian Lee CSP

Check your pulse. Are you human? Do you make mistakes? Of course you are. Of course you do.

I was presenting a major training program for the Ford Motor Company in Michigan. I'd been speaking during the day at the Renaissance Center in Detroit. I had some dinner and then went to the Marriott Hotel in Dearborn to check in.

When I arrived I gave the desk clerk my name and she said, "I'm sorry Mr. Lee, but you don't have a room here."

I said, "No, I have a guaranteed reservation."

She said, "I'm sorry you don't."

Well it had been a long day and I was too tired to argue. So I went over to the pay phone and called my travel agent. She said, "Of course you have a reservation Brian. Here's your confirmation number."

I went back over to the desk, armed with my confirmation number, and a new clerk took over. Her name was Cynthia.

She said, "Mr. Lee, let me check this out." After checking she said, "I'm terribly sorry but we filed your reservation in the wrong month. We will make a room available for you."

She gave me a room. In fact, she upgraded me to a suite. Let me tell you, a suite at the Marriott is oh-so-sweeeeeet.

I bragged about her the next day in my seminar.

Because what Cynthia had done was use "recovery skills." She knew how to, as I like to say: "Mess Up, Fess Up and Dress Up." That's not unusual at Marriott.

I read a newspaper account of another Marriott example, this one in Newton, Mass., where the story said it's not just the manager's job to keep the customers happy. It's everyone's duty.

When a guest is dissatisfied, any associate (the term Marriott uses for its employees) has the authority to make things right.

"We've trained all associates – dishwashers, telephone operators, and housekeepers to listen to guests' wants, then provide whatever allows for complete satisfaction at that first level of complaint. We do this before it gets to managerial level," said Olof Arnheim, the hotel's general manager. "It could be writing off the charge, offering a free meal, another night's lodging, whatever. Our people are quite creative."

Indeed they are.

After one particular couple complained about their meal, the waiter offered them a free dinner the following evening. They were headed home to San Diego the next day, so the waiter offered them dinner at the San Diego Marriott, courtesy of the Newton Marriott.

"They accepted," Arnheim said.

Do we make mistakes? Of course we do. Is there ever going to be a time when we don't make mistakes? Nope!

We're human beings, we're frail, we all make mistakes. Fess up. It's okay to admit that you blew it. So what? Don't blame anyone. Don't point the finger at someone else in your organization; if you make the pointing motion correctly with one extended finger directed at someone else, you may notice that there are also three fingers pointing right back at you!

"Mess Up, Fess Up, Dress Up." With a few exceptions. If you're a heart surgeon, for example, there might be the odd legal complication as a result of "fessing up." You may want to check with Risk Management.

When you mess up and fess up, dress up by doing something just a little bit more than the customer expects.

What do you think it cost the hotel to upgrade me to a suite that night in Dearborn? Maybe a little bit more soap and stuff, but not much. What do you think it did to my loyalty to the company? Lots.

As a matter of fact, I became a Marriott gold card member.

Unfortunately, not all managers have seen the light.

My former office assistant, Candis, was dining with her husband in a gourmet restaurant in Holland – a luxuriously restored 400-year-old stone mill. As the waiter placed her dessert before her (it was a creamy confection in a tall stemmed glass set on a plate) it tipped and spilled – all over her!

The waiter was so busy trying to catch it as it toppled that he forgot about her husband's identical dessert in his other hand and upended that one too, all over him.

Being good sports, they laughed it off as best they could, sponged the stuff off and asked for coffee, secretly hoping they might just get it on the house.

A graceful silver coffee pot arrived in short order on a silver tray, surrounded by petit fours, as well as the bill for the meal, the dessert and $18 for the coffee. The waiter mumbled that he wished he could have done something for them but the manager had already gone home.

Now a good manager would have empowered the waiter to make the call. He should have acknowledged his mistake, given them complimentary dessert and coffee, got their name and address, and the next day sent them a bouquet of flowers.

Don't think word of that kind of service doesn't get around. It does.

Sam Walton, the founder of Wal-Mart, who was one of the richest people in America, knew all about customer service and about dressing up after messing up. He told his people if someone brings back a pair of shoes, give them a new pair and throw in a pair of socks, too. "Give them something for their trouble," he said.

Sometimes, "dress up" might be just a phone call to ask if everything is okay now. Or maybe a baker's dozen. All of us can think of something extra; something just a wee bit creative.

For this to happen, you need two things. You need training, you need trust, and you need to know what to do in the situation.

When you're dealing with customer complaints, there is some good advice worth remembering. It comes from a wonderful organization, Alcoholic's Anonymous.

> *"God grant me the serenity to accept the things I cannot change, the courage to change the things I can and the wisdom to know the difference."*

You can't win 'em all.

With the right training, though, you'll win a lot more than you lose and you'll feel a whole lot better about what you do every day. Plus, you will create customer loyalty.

~ if you look after a customer's problem within the first 24 to 48 hours, 95 percent of them will not only stay with you, but they'll be more loyal to you than ever before. Why? Because they didn't expect it.

The statistics say if you look after a customer's problem within the first 24 to 48 hours, 95 percent of them will not only stay with you, but they'll be more loyal to you than ever before. Why? Because they didn't expect it.

When I was on city council and returned phone calls, people didn't expect it. Many times, they'd forgotten what they'd called to yell at me about. They were always asking me why I'd called them back. People simply aren't used to it.

I delivered a training seminar for a company called Streetside Records where I'd been teaching the importance of "Mess Up, Fess Up, Dress Up."

A few months later, I got a letter from John Mandelker, the owner of the company, that said he'd gone and printed a "License To Please Card," just as I had recommended. He'd given it to every employee. On the card it said, "You can do anything, whatever it takes, to satisfy the customer."

In his letter, he attached rave review letters from several customers.

"While these successes have flowed from a number of changes in management attitude and a new training program," he wrote, "your seminar was a catalyst in getting upper management moving and convincing store management of our serious intent.

"Though you may not remember it, at one point you asked a store manager if she would give away a CD to dress up a problem. After she said she would, you asked me to stand up and state my response.

"It may have been a little hackneyed, but to the managers it was an epiphany. Yes, we have given away several CDs in the last year (18), but December sales were up 22.9 percent on a same-store basis. Thanks."

Take note. Empowering people led to increased sales. John Mandelker is reaping the benefits of training and empowering his people.

The key is, he'd gone back to his place of business and actually done something with his new-found knowledge. Will you?

Chapter 9

Just "D.O. I.T." Checklist

Recommendations:

❑ 1. Practise the Six Star Complaint Golden Rule: "Mess Up, Fess Up, Dress Up."

❑ 2. Make sure you've got the authority to "Dress Up" without having to approach management in advance.

❑ 3. Don't be afraid to use your own good judgement.

$\mathcal{Y}$OUR
ATTITUDE

SECRET #4
"It takes as much time to
shine as it does to whine."

*I*t was the sixth grade. From where I sat, things were going pretty well.

I was getting the third best grades in class and I thought that was good. The prettiest girl in the class got the best grades. She was smart, I was smart. She was pretty, I was – smart.

So I figured we should get together.

I started carrying her books home from school and things were going well. Then I decided, as only sixth-graders can, that it was time for SEX.

Guess what I did? Go ahead, guess.

I kissed her.

Her reaction?

She slugged me.

In the 10th grade, I had a crush on the prettiest girl in the class (again). But I had learned my lesson four years earlier: stay away from the pretty and smart ones. Instead, I concentrated my efforts elsewhere.

I figured I would at least ask this stunning beauty for a dance at the 12th grade prom. But she wasn't there. Why?

Nobody had asked her.

It wasn't until a decade later that I learned about "self-limiting" beliefs in an all-day seminar. It occurred to me that if the only things that were limiting me in life were my own beliefs, then there might be some value in figuring out what they were.

It was the most motivating profound insight I'd ever had to realize that I was in control of my own destiny.

What does this have to do with customer service?

Well, if you seldom experience the kind of customer service you'd like is it possible you have a self-limiting belief that says nobody else is entitled to it either?

When you don't contribute the best that you can to whatever it is you're doing, you're not ripping anybody else off. No, you're ripping yourself off.

Ultimately, what you give out is what you get back from the world. Kind of like a promise.

What do most organizations do? They over-promise and under-deliver.

When I was Vice President and General Manager of a $12 million a year furniture store, one of the hardest things I had ever done was to go out delivering furniture on a truck. Somebody gave me a dollar tip that day and I framed it because I'd worked so hard.

Here I was, a Vice President and I had never even delivered furniture. The reason I went out was because I was fed up. The drivers seldom delivered furniture without damaging it so I went out myself. What I found out was it's pretty hard to deliver furniture without damaging it. You've got to take it on and off trucks, in and around corners, up and down elevators. It gets scratched, dented and stained.

But when our sales people were making the sale, they were promising the furniture would be delivered in perfect condition.

We were over-promising and under-delivering.

I got our salespeople together and I told them, "From now on when you make the sale and get the deposit, tell the customer the furniture will be delivered next Tuesday and it may be damaged, so would you do us a favour and check it over carefully and then call us and we'll send out a repairman."

They were probably going to check it over anyway.

Under-promise, over-deliver.

However, it's not what you say that counts. It's what you do.

Let me repeat it. What you do is what counts, not what you say. People know. Customers know.

The problem is not to educate customers. They know good value. Their perception is bang on. Focus on your behaviour. Take control of your attitude.

Have you ever noticed that some people who are more successful than you, are a whole lot dumber than you? And I'm not just talking about your boss. Think about it. The one ingredient that makes us different is attitude, which has everything to do with our power.

There are three sources of power.

The first is position power, the kind of power held by CEOs, high-ranking politicians and the like.

The second source of power is skills and knowledge. Like they say, knowledge is power. We have now gone from the computer era to the information era and the new billionaires are the ones who produce software programs. Knowledge is power.

The third source of power is what activates the first two; it's the key. It's a sense of mastery. You know that you know. It's called "personal" power.

How do you feel about dealing with someone who has "position" power but no "personal" power? Not good. We avoid them, we go around them, we ignore them, we do everything we can to keep them out of our lives.

Personal power isn't something you're born with. Oh, I guess good genes might help, but you can work on it. The strategy I recommend to increase your personal power consists of three things:

1. Increase your knowledge. If you invest 30 minutes a day in yourself, in five years you'll be a world-class expert. You'll be in the top 20 percent of your field and you know, like I know, that 20 percent of the people make 80 percent of the income.

2. Focus on your behaviour. What you do speaks so loudly most people can't hear what you say.

3. Take control of your attitude. This is not always easy.

Have you ever had one of those days when you flip the alarm clock off and when you next wake up, it's two hours later?

You bolt out of bed, look in the mirror and see that major repair work is required but there isn't time. You slick your hair back, you grab a slice of cold pizza from the fridge, run to the car and when you get on the freeway, you're behind the slowest semi-trailer on the road.

When you arrive at the office, you figure you'll be able to slip in unnoticed but who should be standing there waiting but the boss. Tapping her toe. You know it's going to be a bad day.

The only thing worse than working with someone who's having a bad day is working with someone who has a bad day, every day. They do have one thing going for them, at least they're consistent. Your attitude is up and down like a yo-yo.

I have read the Bible, I have read the Koran and the Veda and in no source of wisdom can I find a God who creates bad days. So who does?

Look in the mirror. It's not your customer!

There are three ways to get control of your attitude.

Number one, check your self-talk.

At any given moment, ask yourself what outcome you'd like in a situation and go for it. Don't take the bait. Don't be had.

My friend Ciro in Houston said to me, "Brian, I love it when employees bring me angry customers."

"Why?" I said.

"Because," he replied with a smile, "I nice them – to death."

Take your customer's problem seriously. Don't take it personally. Check your self-talk.

Number two, be aware of your self-limiting beliefs.

Number three, ask yourself if you're more concerned about yourself or your customer.

My brother and I went to our general insurance broker, Hyder, a few months ago because we thought we needed more insurance. I told him to give us the disability insurance we needed and as usual I gave him a blank cheque. That's how much I trust him.

But he didn't provide the disability insurance. When I asked about it, he said our company is so small that it would cost more than it was worth. He suggested we join the chamber of commerce and take advantage of a group plan.

If you know anything about the insurance business, then you know how much commission he walked away from. You might even think he's nuts!

But who was he really concerned about?

That's right, his customer. He gave the best advice for me and, in the long run, for himself.

By the way, over 100 of his clients are my relatives, friends and staff.

The biggest killer of relationships is ego and the easiest way to get ego out of the way is to change your focus – to focus your efforts on the customer.

If attitude was contagious, would you want anybody to catch yours? Is attitude contagious? It's epidemic.

Most of us operate at just a small fraction of our capability. I believe there is nothing you couldn't accomplish in your life if it weren't for one very dangerous practise you may engage in from time to time – the morning coffee break "Ain't it awful" club.

"Ain't it awful we have to read this book?"

"Ain't it awful about the economy?"

"Ain't it awful, ain't it awful, ain't it awful?"

What happens is, even if you've always thought of yourself as a pretty positive person, in order to be accepted by your "Ain't it awful" buddies down at work, you've got to believe it's awful, too.

Then what happens is, instead of treating the customer with TLC (Tender Loving Care), we begin to treat them with TDC (Thinly Disguised Contempt).

You can joke about anything you want to, but don't joke about customers because that's what you're all about. While we're at it, get rid of the silly cartoons pinned up around the office.

We all laugh, just as we used to laugh (and some unfortunately still do) at racial and ethnic slurs. The hidden meaning is frightening. Behind the cuteness is an attitude of contempt for your customers.

Attitude is everything.

It is the highest and best expression of us. Norman Vincent Peale has said, "It is the priceless quality that makes everything different."

What value are your customer service skills without the attitude that says you are, indeed, going to make it happen?

Go back to the list in chapter four, the list of what you expect as customers. It is almost all attitude.

It was Henry Ford, a man I admire very much, who said this:

> *"You can do anything if you have enthusiasm.*
>
> *Enthusiasm is the yeast that makes your hope rise to the stars.*
>
> *Enthusiasm is the sparkle in your eye, it is the swing in your gait, the grip of your hand, the irresistible surge of your will and the energy to execute your ideas.*
>
> *Enthusiasts are fighters.*
>
> *They have fortitude.*
>
> *They have strong qualities.*
>
> *Enthusiasm is at the bottom of all progress – with it, there is accomplishment, without it, there are only alibis."*

Put the power of your attitude to work.

Ask yourself, next time you're dealing with a difficult customer, how by taking control of your own personal power you could have made your customer's day?

Chapter 10

Just "D.O. I.T." Checklist

Recommendations:

❑ 1. Remember "It takes as much time to shine as it does to whine." Even less much less.

❑ 2. Discover your own "self-limiting beliefs," towards yourself and your customers. Don't short-change either.

❑ 3. Invest 30 minutes a day in personal education.

❑ 4. Focus on your behaviour. What you do speaks so loudly, most people can't hear what you say.

❑ 5. Take control of your attitude by asking yourself, "Am I more concerned about myself or my customer?"

❑ 6. When dealing with really negative customers don't "take the bait." Take the problem seriously, not personally.

❑ 7. Resign from the "Ain't it awful" club.

❑ 8. Treat your customers with "TLC" (Tender Loving Care).

PEOPLE

SECRET #5
"To guarantee customers get
what they expect, recognize and
celebrate exceptional service
to show your respect."

A simple thank you.

It requires so little effort. But in all my years of training, I have yet to come across a company that has properly thanked its people. Do you remember the last time your boss thanked you for looking after your customers well? Count yourself lucky if you do.

When I began my contract with Ford, I was designing a training program for 3,200 people and I met with a group of executives trying to decide what they needed most.

I said to them, "Give me some examples of employees who have gone above and beyond the call of duty."

They just sat there, looking bewildered.

"Do you know anybody?"

"I don't know anybody. Do you know anybody?"

"Not me. Do you know anybody?"

This bothered them so much, they "put a man on it." They actually assigned somebody to search for examples of good customer service within their division.

What I discovered two years later, after delivering the program, was that there were now 3,200 associates who acted above and beyond the call of duty. I found heroic examples everywhere. But they had to have someone do the research, because their corporate culture did not support acknowledging people for good behaviour.

Never underestimate the power of a well-placed thank you.

In my seminars, I do something that consistently blows people away. I pick a local hero, I bring him/her up on stage, talk a little about the individual's accomplishments and then we give a standing ovation.

It's marvelous. Imagine it for one minute and see how you feel.

One day while on the east coast I took volunteers from the audience. I wasn't setting it up in advance, just taking volunteers. I didn't tell them why they were coming up and I didn't know anything about them ahead of time.

I picked a middle-aged man out of the audience; he came up on stage and we gave him a standing ovation. It was great as usual.

He waited and came up to me at the end of the seminar and said, "Mr. Lee, I don't know why you're here today and I wasn't quite sure why I came. You had no way of knowing this when you called me to the front, but I was recently in a car accident: my car was wiped out. I had no insurance. I lost my job three weeks ago. My wife left me, took my two children, and my aunt is dying.

"That acknowledgement was exactly what I needed in my life."

When it comes to employees, we just don't say thanks.

This is what empowerment really means. It is seeing the gifts and the talents, the caring and the intelligence in another person and helping them live up to that.

Michael LeBoeuf, in his book *The Greatest Management Principle in the World,* said, "Things that get recognized and rewarded, get repeated."

Recognize good behaviour and it will get repeated. Recognize bad behaviour and guess what happens? If you have kids, you know they'll do anything to get attention. Just start recognizing people for doing things approximately right and watch out how quickly it returns.

Besides, you'll feel great doing it.

Chapter 11

Just "D.O. I.T." Checklist

Recommendations:

❏ 1. Seek every opportunity to acknowledge your peers for exceptional customer service.

❏ 2. Whenever possible, thank co-workers in front of others.

❏ 3. Invite your customers to nominate customer superstars.

❏ 4. Take the initiative to establish a formal awards and recognition team.

CHAPTER 12

$\mathcal{E}$XCELLENCE

SECRET #6
"The secret of personal and
professional excellence is to
'learn one new idea every day
and do it in a better way.' "

*W*hen I travel the world and tell people where I come from, I don't have to explain where Calgary is anymore. I don't have to tell them it's in the province of Alberta, just north of Montana.

My home town hit the map in 1988.

That's when the Winter Olympics were held in Calgary and that event probably did more for our city than anything else. There was one particular event going on during the Olympics that really stands out for me.

Figure skating.

You'd watch figure skaters perform on the ice at the Olympic Saddledome and give a fantastic performance. The crowd would love it. Everyone in the building would be energized by their greatness.

Then the camera would pan down to the face of the skater as they waited for their marks. You'd often see sadness; the tears streaming down their cheeks.

As good as it seemed to us in the audience, they knew it was not their best.

Other times, a performance wouldn't be anywhere near medal standard. In fact, the marks might be downright lousy. Yet the skater was beaming with pride. They knew they'd skated as well as they possibly could.

That, folks, is the concept of excellence; the concept of being the best you can be, the concept of knowing inside you've done absolutely everything you could possibly do.

Who do world-class competitors really compete against? Themselves.

In pursuit of excellence I want to share with you this theme: "Anything you can do, you can do better."

We are into the age of quality. It has almost become a movement. Quality is one of the buzz words of the 1990s. Ford is famous for its slogan, "Quality is Job One."

What is total quality?

A term many are using is "zero defects."

What is excellence?

As Jan Carlzon, the President of Scandinavian Airlines, said: "It is not doing one thing 1,000 percent better. Rather, it's doing a thousand things one percent better." I doubt there is any single thing in your place of work that you could do 1,000 percent better. If there is, it must be brand new or pretty awful right now.

I'd be willing to wager there are plenty of things you could do one percent better. And better, and better, and better.

Excellence is an obsession with the little things that matter to your patrons. It almost borders on a fanaticism with the little things that are important.

I saw a bumper sticker a few years ago that said, "The little things in life don't mean anything."

How stupid is that?

I can't imagine anyone would have paid two bucks for anything that said that. I had dinner with my mother last year and she said to me, "Why is it that when your twin brother Bruce (She didn't say twin brother Bruce. She knows he's my twin. I just put that in there for your benefit.) sends me a card, he just signs his name and when you send me a card, you write me a little note?"

I said, "Oh mother. There are more important things in the world to worry about than that."

She said, "No there isn't."

Who's right?

Well first of all, mothers are always right. This was no exception. Is it the big things that are important in our relationships or is it the little things? I think it's the little things.

By the way, the reason I always write a note is because I'm rarely in town when my mother needs me and my brother Bruce is usually there for her. There's a little bit of guilt involved.

It's the little things that count.

Have you ever noticed when you're flying on an airplane and you go to the bathroom, it is virtually impossible to keep the toilet seat up? Whenever there's a slight hint of turbulence, you've got a real mess to deal with. Couldn't somebody come up with a little gadget to keep the seat up?

How about a hook, or velcro, or maybe hire someone to hold it up!

It's the little things that count.

Or how about when you get a flyer in your mailbox advertising some gizmo on sale for 97 cents. The little old lady who lives next door takes three buses and goes all across town only to arrive at the store and be told the item is out of stock? It happens all the time.

Little thing or big thing?

Have you ever noticed when you take your clothes to the dry-cleaners, they have to have some kind of identification so the clothes don't get lost? Fair enough. But do they have to staple it to my shirts?

I had a dry-cleaner that I used to spend $125 a month with that hasn't yet figured out that you don't have to actually staple it to the shirt.

I phoned him once and complained and he said he would solve it. I phoned him a second time and he blamed it on the staff. I phoned him a third time and I said cancel my credit card account, I'm not doing business with you anymore.

He didn't quite figure out that this little thing made all the difference in the world to me. There are at least 200 dry-cleaners in the city of Calgary, 20 of them deliver to the home and I didn't need him.

Chances are in your business, it's the little things that make a difference too.

Excellence is daily continuous improvement.

I was speaking at my association of professional speakers in Calgary not too long ago and afterwards, a friend came up to me and said, "Brian, I can't believe how much you've improved since I heard you last."

"I better have," I replied. "I've spoken 250 times since you heard me last."

What I love about what I do is every day I get to add new ideas from the newspapers and magazines I've read or the people I've met.

Do you have five years, 10 years or 25 years of experience in your line of work? Or do you have one year of experience in your field just repeated five, 10 or 25 times?

The world is changing. Our customers are demanding more, demanding better. What they understand is value.

Could you go back to your office tomorrow and do one thing, one percent better? Could you go back the next day and make your desk one percent neater? Could you go in the day after that and communicate with your people one percent better? How many days in a row could you do one thing one percent better?

Is this believable? Is this achievable?

In the course of a year, how much more valuable would you be to your employer, to your organization, to yourself? You see, it **is** the little things that count.

Excellence is nothing more than being absolutely the best you can be. What is the alternative? Let me tell you it's not all that attractive. It's mediocrity. It's being average. Or as a former girlfriend used to describe me – adequate.

Just because everyone else is satisfied to be average in their business doesn't mean you have to be, too.

In our company, we are continually updating the programs that we do. Sometimes, I think it drives the office staff crazy with the continual changes. When you go to a seminar or read a book, I hardly think you want to read yesterday's ideas.

So we try to get better all the time.

Irving Berlin wrote a famous song called, "Anything you can do, I can do better."

I liked the music but not the words so I rewrote them.

Anything You Can Do, YOU Can Do Better!

"I can do whatever, just a little better. Aiming to aspire, just a little higher. Adequate is not enough. The mission for me is the best I can be."

My guess is, it could be a mission statement for you and your organization.

Let me make one thing clear however. Excellence is not perfection. Perfection is looking for what's wrong. Excellence is looking for what's right.

A perfectionist can never be done, can never be finished, can never get anything exactly right. What I observed many years ago is that if you stay at the office long enough to get everything done just right, you will never go home. And if you do go home, you'll never leave the job at the office.

Excellence says you can celebrate today. It may not be perfect but you can celebrate because it's better than it was yesterday. You know what? Tomorrow is going to be better still.

We've all heard that old expression, "If it's worth doing, it's worth doing right."

I like to look at that just a little differently and say, "If it's worth doing, it's worth doing poorly the first time."

Say what?

I had an associate working in my office a number of years ago who believed you could not go out and give a speech unless everything was perfect. Perfect content. Perfect illustrations. Perfect everything.

Nine years later, this man has yet to get his public speaking career going.

I remember my first seminar.

The content was embarrassing. My delivery skills were doubtful. The one thing I had going for myself was my enthusiasm and my passion for the subject. What matters is I got started and I got better.

Meanwhile, my associate was planning to analyze, to think about it, to study, to consider, to ponder, to review, and he never did get off the fence and get going.

My point is, the plan you have for improving your customer service may not be perfect, but go ahead and do it anyway. If it's worth doing, it's worth doing poorly.

One of the biggest successes in retailing today is the wholesale warehouse. Costco and Sam's Warehouse (a division of Wal-Mart) are revolutionizing the retail market and the average store does $75 million worth of business every year.

What they understand is they have to continuously change 25 percent of their stock so people will have a sense of excitement, a sense of anticipation, when they return. Maybe there's something we can learn from that.

In the 2000s, maybe we shouldn't just learn from our mistakes, maybe we should learn from other people's successes. My guess is success lies in doing something you haven't done before.

I know it's a cliché, but if you "Keep doing what you've been doing, you'll keep getting what you've got." Is that good enough?

I have a hairstylist who is often whining. People ask me why I keep going to him. Well it's because he did a great deal to get me elected in politics a decade ago and I've never forgotten about that. I'm loyal.

He continuously complains that all his customers ever talk about is price. Yet if you look in the yellow pages, what does he advertise? Price. Go outside the front door and check out the portable sign. Price. What has he done differently in the past five years in his shop? Nothing. Nada. Zero.

He can't understand, when he adds up his receipts, why the total is still the same.

Keep doing what you've been doing and you'll keep getting what you've got.

Vince Lombardi, that great motivator who coached the National Football League's Green Bay Packers into immortality, said this:

The quality of a person's life is in direct proportion to his commitment to excellence, regardless of his chosen field of endeavour.

I have not found a field of endeavour, or a job, that could not benefit from this concept of continuous improvement.

If there is a hell, surely it must be doing the same thing, working at the same job, doing it the same way over and over and over again.

As one of my fellow speakers, Mark Victor Hansen, said, "The genius of goals is once you commit to a goal, you already have it. It just hasn't arrived yet."

A few years ago, I lost 35 pounds. It took me six months but I had it licked, not after the 35 pounds was gone, I had it licked the moment I made the commitment.

LET ME SUMMARIZE FOR YOU THE 12 ATTRIBUTES OF EXCELLENCE.

1 Replace perfectionism with excellence.

Replace an old bad habit with a new good habit. It takes 21 days to form a habit. Those first few days on my diet were tough. The first day, I had to go to bed at 6:30 p.m. because I was so used to having a sugar fix between meals that I'd become exhausted.

After three weeks, after 21 days, my new habits were starting to take root.

2 Love what you do.

How do you know if you love what you do? Ask yourself, can people tell if you are working or playing? Would you get up in the morning and do what you do if you didn't get paid for it?

I was presenting a seminar to car sales representatives. At the end, I asked everyone to get up and tell us the one thing they got out of the seminar that was most important to them.

One young guy got up and said, "Brian, am I ever glad you said that. I hate selling. I hate cars. I'm going to quit."

His sales manager was sitting next to him. He got up and said, "Am I ever glad to hear that. He wasn't any good anyway."

Now at least that young man could go somewhere and do something that he loved or at least liked to do, and his old job was available for someone who loved to sell cars.

More than 80 percent of people work at jobs they don't like or that are mismatched for their talents. What a sad commentary, using all the energy you have during the day doing something that you don't like and then using whatever energy you have left over at the end of the day and on the weekends to do what you do want to do.

That doesn't sound like a worthwhile life experience to me.

If you find yourself whining and complaining, it's time to move on or change your attitude. Maybe this is not a bad time to think about that.

3 Stand for something.

What do you stand for personally in life? What is your passion? What do you believe in?

A while ago there was a show on television about people who had lived to be 100 years old. One of the concepts they talked about was "engagement." These people had something they believed in, something they wanted to do with their lives and it helped them withstand the pain of all their friends and family around them dying.

As Jack Palance said to Billy Crystal in the movie "City Slickers," when asked what the key to life was, "Have one thing in life that you believe in so much, nothing else matters."

My guess is we all have that one thing, that passion. What is the one thing that you stand for, above and beyond which or about which nobody else may joke?

81

4 Make a commitment.

Do people know what you believe in? Make a commitment.

"Commitment is what transforms a promise into reality. It is the words that speak boldly of your intentions and the actions which speak louder than words. It is making the time when there is none. It is coming through time after time, year after year. Commitment is the stuff character is made of, the power to change the face of things that are. It is the daily triumph of integrity over skepticism." – Anonymous

5 Expect the best.

What I've noticed about most people is they expect the worst and they end up being right. Try expecting the best for a change.

I was at a convention of professional speakers in Orlando and I had just heard that great motivator, Anthony Robbins, speak. After the speech, there was a big crowd waiting for the elevators to go up to their rooms between sessions.

As I'm standing there waiting for the elevator, this woman standing next to me, a professional speaker who motivates people for a living says, "These elevators are never going to come."

"Excuse me," I said. "They certainly are going to come."

Expect the best. You just might get it.

6 Commit to the concept of continuous learning.

We need to keep looking for new ideas; we need to keep learning. When was the last time you went to a seminar on customer service? Do you know what the latest developments are in your business?

7 "When the student is ready, the teacher appears." – Bible

This is a very important concept. It is the idea of the teachable moment. When you are ready to find the answer, it is there. But you've got to be ready and open to receive it.

8 Adopt a mentor.

Find someone who knows more than you do; someone you admire and respect in your field of endeavour; someone you could sit down with from time to time and say, "How do you do that?" What I've noticed about successful people is they love to share their ideas.

9 Don't let the things you cannot control interfere with the things you can.

I'm not saying don't be concerned about the rest of the world, because you should be. What I am saying is focus on what you can do, not on what you can't do. This is an important concept and it's not just semantics. It's not just, "Is the glass half empty or is the glass half full?"

Rick Hansen went fishing one day and on his way home he was riding in the back of a truck that overturned. When he woke up, he was in the hospital and he had lost the use of his legs. He heard constantly about what he couldn't do.

Rick Hansen focused on what he could do, and he went on to circle the world by wheelchair, becoming an inspiration to millions and raising $26 million in the process.

10 Ask yourself at the end of every day what you did today that could make your job easier tomorrow?

What did I change today that will make it easier to do my job and serve other people tomorrow?

11 Create a pocket of excellence.

As Tom Peters says, "You may not change the world, but create a pocket of excellence." Let what you do stand as a symbol for everybody else. It takes exactly the same amount of time to shine as it does to whine. As a matter of fact, it takes less time to shine than it does to whine because if you whine, you've got to do it over and over and over again. If you solve the problem, you can move on to the next one.

Dr. Leo Buscaglia, "Doctor Love," said, "Live every day as if it's your last. You never know when you're going to be right."

12 Act with urgency.

When you get a good idea, act on it now. Banish the phrase, "I'll try," from your vocabulary. Don't try. Just do it!

What are you doing in your life today, even if you're not working, that is contributing to and helping other people?

The moment you make a commitment is the moment when change takes place.

Make that commitment:

To your customers to live up to their expectations by living up to the expectations that you have for yourself.

To communication. To remembering that how you communicate with your customers is everything and remembering that it has very little to do with what you say and everything to do with what you do and how you do it.

To systems. To ensure that you understand why people complain and that you will "Mess Up, Fess Up and Dress Up."

To attitude. It is the foundation of success in every form of human endeavour and it is everything in customer service.

To each other. To recognize and celebrate your people and let them know how much you appreciate them.

To continuous improvement. Which is nothing more than living up to your potential as a human being and growing into it just a little bit more each day.

Because the alternative – a life of mediocrity – is simply not worth your time.

Chapter 12

Just "D.O. I.T." Checklist

Recommendations:

❏ 1. Focus on doing 1,000 things, one percent better.

❏ 2. Learn one new idea every day, and do it in a better way.

❏ 3. Commit to excellence, being the best you can be.

❏ 4. Practice the 12 Attributes of Excellence:

    1. Replace perfectionism with excellence.

    2. Love what you do.

    3. Stand for something.

    4. Make a commitment.

    5. Expect the best.

    6. Commit to continuous learning.

    7. When the student is ready, the teacher appears.

    8. Adopt a mentor.

    9. Don't let the things you cannot control, interfere with the things you can.

    10. Ask yourself at the end of every day – "How did I improve today?"

    11. Create a pocket of excellence.

    12. Act with urgency.

*M*AKING
A DIFFERENCE

"Life Changes:
*not when we **begin** to act*
*but when we **commit** to act"*
– Brian Lee CSP

*T*hey say there are no heroes anymore. Well I still have one.

His name is Joey Smallwood and he was the man who brought Newfoundland into Canada in 1949.

Several years ago, he was speaking in Calgary to a convention of the Urban Municipalities Associations. He got a standing ovation, too. A remarkable man he was, even then at the ripe old age of 80.

The chairman of the event came over to me afterwards and asked, "Brian, would you mind finding someone to drive Mr. Smallwood to the airport?"

I said, "Would I? I'll drive him."

I got him into the car and since I wanted to have a talk with him, I took the long way. As I was driving, I gave him a copy of a Calgary magazine with an article about me in which I'd said that he was one of my heroes.

I said, "Mr. Smallwood, I've admired you, I've read your biography, I've read your autobiography. You must have been the most vilified person in all of Newfoundland because when you brought Newfoundland into Confederation you were considered a traitor by half the population. You've been attacked for everything.

"I've been in politics for six years and I still find it very uncomfortable to know that people whom I've never met hate my guts. You think I've got a tough skin? No way. How did you do it?"

Well, when Joey Smallwood answers a question he tends to go on and on and on. (Good thing I took the circuitous route.)

Finally he said, "You know Brian, not everybody can change the world; not everybody can bring a province into Confederation. As bad as it got, I had to remember the song I learned in Sunday School: Brighten the Corner Where You Are."

Brighten the Corner Where You Are – we're not talking about changing the world here.

We're talking about doing what we do because we love to do it. Yes, we want to make our own day. We have the opportunity by what we say, by how we say it, by what we do, by how we do it, and by the product and service we provide to make someone else's day, too. All that matters is that you brought that little bit extra to help other people feel good about themselves.

This is the highest motivation we can all aspire to – the motivation to serve others.

Someone once said, "Service is the rent we pay for the space we occupy" and I don't even think it's rent. It's the most wonderful thing we can do.

My challenge to you is to manage your time and to manage your customers' "Moments of Truth" (a term coined by Jan Carlzon, the President of Scandinavian Airlines).

Most of all, to brighten the corner where you are.

These are the Six Secrets of Six Star Customer Satisfaction; secrets that will help you, too, to satisfy every customer, every time, and as a result enhance your career and create Satisfaction Guaranteed!

Chapter 13

Just "D.O. I.T." Checklist

Recommendations:

❏　1.　Brighten the corner where you are!

❏　2.　Practise the six secrets of lifetime customer loyalty.

❏　3.　Pass this book on to a friend.

❏　4.　Complete the "Reader Satisfaction Survey" at the back of the book and let me know how I can serve you better.

　　　　　– Brian Lee CSP

$\mathscr{A}$DDENDA

91

Mission:
How to create lifetime
customer loyalty

Value #1 "Your Customer"

1. SECRET #1 "Just consistently meet your customers' expectations (both external and internal) and your customers will make you a star."

2. Service excellence is a passion for the intangibles.

Value #2 "Communication"

3. SECRET #2 "Customers judge you by: the way you look; what you say; how you say it; what you do; how you do it."

4. Know how to read your customers and how they read you. Words = 7%; Tone of Voice = 38%; Non-verbal = 55%

Value #3 "Systems"

5. SECRET #3 "What I believe doesn't count, what my customer perceives does."

   Perception = Deception

6. Customers want a personal, timely, commitment from problem solvers. 68% do not return because of an attitude of indifference.

7. Practise recovery skills: "Mess up, Fess up, and Dress up." Remember only one out of 26 customers will bother to complain.

Value #4 "Attitude"

8. To enhance your personal power:

   ◆ increase your knowledge

     ◆ focus upon your behaviour

       ◆ take control of your attitude.

   SECRET #4 "It takes as much time to shine as it does to whine."

9. Check your self-talk.

10. Be aware of your self-limiting beliefs.

Value #5 "Your People"

11. Practise the greatest management principle in the world: "Things that get recognized and rewarded get repeated" – Michael LeBoeuf

    SECRET #5 "To guarantee customers get what they expect, recognize and celebrate exceptional service to show your respect."

Value #6 "Quality Product/Service"

12. "It is not doing one thing 1,000 percent better. Rather, it is doing a thousand things one percent better."

13. Make a commitment to being the best you can be.

14. Ask yourself at the end of every day:

    "What did I do today that will improve service to my customers tomorrow?"

    SECRET #6 The secret of personal and professional excellence is to: "Learn one new idea every day and do it in a better way."

The following questions reflect the critical concepts covered in the Satisfaction Guaranteed™ Seminar Series. Circle your TRUE or FALSE answer.

WORLD-CLASS CUSTOMER SATISFACTION STRATEGY

True   False   1. The key strategy for creating a long-term competitive advantage is to consistently meet your customers' expectations.

True   False   2. It is more important to give priority to external customers ahead of internal customers.

True   False   3. The hospitality industry's five-star rating system is based upon the quality of service provided to customers.

True   False   4. Value = Quality + Service + Price.

True   False   5. All things being equal, it is customer service that differentiates individuals and organizations from their competitors.

SATISFACTION GUARANTEED

True   False   6. Real customer satisfaction comes from how well we provide the tangibles (i.e., product or service), as opposed to the intangibles (feelings about the service received).

True   False   7. The actual words we use in communicating with customers make up over 50 percent of the impact.

True   False   8. It's OK to take the blame for a complaint from a customer even if it really wasn't your fault.

True   False   9. What we believe about our product or service doesn't matter but what our customer perceives does.

True   False   10. When serving customers our attitude is even more important than aptitude or technical competence.

True   False   11. It is not necessary to recognize or acknowledge individuals for providing good customer service, as long as they are well paid.

True   False   12. Excellence is doing one thing 1,000 percent better.

(Answers on next page.)

SATISFACTION GUARANTEED SELF-TEST ANSWERS

1.   True

2.   True

3.   False

4.   False

5.   True

6.   False

7.   False

8.   True

9.   True

10.   True

11.   False

12.   False

SIX STAR™
COMPLAINT/SUGGESTION TRACKING LOG

Document every customer complaint, suggestion or request for information on a daily basis in order to be able to track "trends" and create permanent solutions.

Dept.

Date	#	Resolved		Complaint/Suggestion	Identified by:
	1.	Yes	No		
	2.	Yes	No		
	3.	Yes	No		
	4.	Yes	No		
	5.	Yes	No		
	6.	Yes	No		
	7.	Yes	No		
	8.	Yes	No		
	9.	Yes	No		
	10.	Yes	No		

Just "D.O. I.T." Team Workshop Agenda

(Daily Ongoing Implementation Tactics)

◆ Team Name:_____

◆ Meeting Day_____ Date_____ Begin_____ Adjourn_____
   (Note: To take place within 48 hours of the most recent seminar)

◆ Team Member Invitation List_____
   _____

◆ Additional Guests_____
   _____

◆ Action Planning on Seminar Title_____

◆ Agenda Attachment – copy of Seminar Just D.O. I.T. Checklist

◆ Members to Bring – Their seminar workbooks and BEST IDEAS!

1. Call to Order _____
   Chaired by S.E.A. (Service Excellence Advisor)

2. Team Member Debrief
Each team member in attendance shares what they feel were the
   best ideas gained from the most recent seminar.
Notes:

3. Seminar Recommendations
Team members review the specific recommendations from
the seminar and determine:
a) Ideas that will be acted upon NOW
b) Ideas that will be followed up by a TASK GROUP or
   Future Workshop
Notes:

4. Ideas Arising

Team members may bring up any other ideas they gained or developed from the seminar.

Notes:

5. Empowerment to Others

How can these concepts, ideas and implementation strategies be extended to all personnel (not attending seminars)?

6. Brag Fair

Is the team ready to select its project to enter in the BRAG FAIR and AWARDS CEREMONY?

Date: _____ Location: _____

7. Next Seminar

Clarify and confirm next seminar:

a) Date: _____ Time: _____

   Location: _____

b) Team member attendance

c) Who else should be attending? _____

_____

8. Next Just D.O. I.T. Workshop

Date: _____ Time: _____

Location: _____

9. Good of the Team

Each team member offers a final comment, suggestion or criticism (along with a constructive suggestion for improvement), that they believe will enhance the good of the team.

10. Adjourn

$\mathcal{J}$UST D.O. I.T. CHECKLIST SUMMARY

Foreward – Just "D.O. I.T." Checklist

❑ 1. Conduct a "best practices" tour and visit the three organizations in your market area that are famous for "world-class" customer satisfaction. Ask a lot of questions.

❑ 2. Invest in yourself. Take a minimum of 18 hours a year in Customer Service-related training.

❑ 3. Whatever inspires you in this book, act on it URGENTLY. Ideas have a way of "cooling down" over time.

Chapter 1 – Just "D.O. I.T." Checklist

❑ 1. Smile and make eye contact. Say "please and thank you." Be a model for everyone.

❑ 2. Treat every customer as a friend. Better still as an "honoured visitor."

❑ 3. Don't underestimate the importance of your "telephone voice." Speak softly, as if you were at home.

Chapter 2 — Just "D.O. I.T." Checklist

❏ 1. Treat anyone you provide a service to as your customer, including your boss and co-workers.

❏ 2. Make a list of your various types of customers and ask them "What can I do to serve you better?"

❏ 3. Serve others the way you'd like to be served.

Chapter 3 — Just "D.O. I.T." Checklist

❏ 1. For a three-month period, calculate the cost of acquiring new customers. Let everybody know.

❏ 2. The fastest way to improve your job/career satisfaction is to improve your customer satisfaction.

❏ 3. Act as if you were a "consultant" to your customer. Don't "suggest" . . . "recommend."

❏ 4. Work with your team to set specific, measurable goals for customer satisfaction. Share them with everyone.

Chapter 4 — Just "D.O. I.T." Checklist

❏ 1. Make a list of all of your customer's expectations. Prioritize the top six and do whatever it takes to meet them.

❏ 2. Be sincere! (Whether you mean it or not.)

❑ 3. It's OK to be friendly. As a minimum, be professional.

❑ 4. Get to know where everything is and what everyone does. Your customers expect it.

❑ 5. Don't make your customers adapt to you. Adapt to them.

❑ 6. Smile. It's contagious (except when removing stitches).

❑ 7. Make an effort to remember and recognize your customers.

❑ 8. Practice good grooming habits. Toothbrush and mouthwash are tools of your trade.

❑ 9. Anticipate.

❑ 10. Focus on the intangibles.

Chapter 5 – Just "D.O. I.T." Checklist

❑ 1. Make a commitment to consistently deliver the "Six Star" values of lifetime customer loyalty.

❑ 2. Ask yourself every day before you start work, "If attitude were contagious, would I want anyone to catch mine?"

❑ 3. Consider the customer in everything that you do.

Chapter 6 — Just "D.O. I.T." Checklist

❏ 1. Be aware that customers "read you" non-verbally within the first seven seconds of contact.

❏ 2. Be certain you read your customers.

❏ 3. Watch out for emotional deaf spots – what your customers don't like about you.

Chapter 7 — Just "D.O. I.T." Checklist

❏ 1. Practice the two rules of Customer Satisfaction

Rule No. 1: The customer is always right

Rule No. 2: When the customer is wrong, see rule number one.

❏ 2. Be aware that we usually see ourselves differently than our customers do. It takes about 100 days to grow "blinders."

❏ 3. Make darn sure your customer doesn't leave you because of an attitude of indifference.

Chapter 8 — Just "D.O. I.T." Checklist

❏ 1. Never say "it's policy." Give the reason for the policy.

❏ 2. If you cannot find the reason for a policy, it's probably a "Sacred Cow." Change it. Besides, "Sacred Cows" make great steaks.

❏ 3. Make sure you communicate a "can do," not a "can't do" attitude.

Chapter 9 – Just "D.O. I.T." Checklist

❏ 1. Practise the Six Star Complaint Golden Rule "Mess Up, Fess Up, Dress Up."

❏ 2. Make sure you've got the authority to "Dress Up" without having to approach management in advance.

❏ 3. Don't be afraid to use your own good judgement.

Chapter 10 – Just "D.O. I.T." Checklist

❏ 1. Remember "It takes as much time to shine as it does to whine." Even less, much less.

❏ 2. Discover your own "self-limiting beliefs," towards yourself and your customers. Don't short-change either.

❏ 3. Invest 30 minutes a day in personal education.

❏ 4. Focus on your behaviour. What you do speaks so loudly, most people can't hear what you say.

❏ 5. Take control of your attitude by asking yourself, "Am I more concerned about myself or my customer?"

❏ 6. When dealing with really negative customers don't "take the bait." Take the problem seriously, not personally.

❏ 7. Resign from the "Ain't it awful" club.

❏ 8. Treat your customers with "TLC" (Tender Loving Care).

Chapter 11 – Just "D.O. I.T." Checklist

❑ 1. Seek every opportunity to acknowledge your peers for exceptional customer service.

❑ 2. Whenever possible, thank co-workers in front of others.

❑ 3. Invite your customers to nominate customer superstars.

❑ 4. Take the initiative to establish a formal awards and recognition team.

Chapter 12 – Just "D.O. I.T." Checklist

❑ 1. Focus on doing 1,000 things, one percent better.

❑ 2. Learn one new idea every day, and do it in a better way.

❑ 3. Commit to excellence, being the best you can be.

❑ 4. Practice the 12 Attributes of Excellence:
1. Replace perfectionism with excellence.
2. Love what you do.
3. Stand for something.
4. Make a commitment.
5. Expect the best.
6. Commit to continuous learning.
7. When the student is ready, the teacher appears.
8. Adopt a mentor.

9. Don't let the things you cannot control, interfere with the things you can.

10. Ask yourself at the end of every day – "How did I improve today?"

11. Create a pocket of excellence.

12. Act with urgency.

Chapter 13 – Just "D.O. I.T." Checklist

❑ 1. Brighten the corner where you are!

❑ 2. Practise the six secrets of lifetime customer loyalty.

❑ 3. Pass this book onto a friend.

❑ 4. Complete the "Reader Satisfaction Survey" at the back of the book and let me know how I can serve you better.

– Brian Lee CSP

SIX STAR™
RECOMMENDED READING

Satisfaction Guaranteed™

1. Customers for Life, Carl Sewell and Paul Brown, Simon & Schuster, Inc., 1990

2. The 7 Habits of Highly Effective People, Stephen R. Covey, Simon & Schuster, Inc., 1990

Winning With Difficult Customers

3. I'm OK, You're OK, Thomas Harris, M.D., Avon Books, 1973, Summit Books, 1991

4. Awake the Giant Within, Anthony Robbins, Summit Books, 1993

Stress-Free Service Excellence

5. Stress for Success, Peter Hanson, Collins Publishers, 1989

6. Peak Performers, Charles Garfield, William Morrow and Company, 1986

One Minute Service Selling

7. One Minute Sales Person, Larry Wilson, Avon, 1981

8. How to Sell Anything to Anybody, Joe Girard, Warent, 1984

Managing Moments of Truth

9. <u>How to Win Customers and Keep Them for Life</u>, Michael LeBoeuf, G.P. Putnam's Sons, 1987

10. <u>Moments of Truth</u>, Jan Carlzon, Harper & Row, 1989

Self-Esteem and Service Superstars

11. <u>Think and Grow Rich</u> (revised edition), Napoleon Hill, Fawcett Crest, 1960

12. <u>The Road Less Traveled</u>, M. Scott Peck, Simon & Schuster, 1985

More Good Books

13. <u>5th Discipline</u>, Peter Senge

14. <u>Raving fans</u>, Ken Blanchard and Sheldon Bowleskh

Superlearning Music

◆ Pachelbel Canon in D. Hari Singh Khalsa & Gary Sill, 1985 Invincible Music (Canada) Socan. GRO Recordings, Vancouver, B.C.

◆ Black & White, Danny Wright, Nichols-Weight Records (817) 476-1140

CUSTOMER RESPONSIVENESS/ PROFESSIONAL DEVELOPMENT

ROFILE OF AN
AUTHOR AND
WORLD-CLASS
PROFESSIONAL
SPEAKER

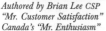

Authored by Brian Lee CSP
"Mr. Customer Satisfaction"
Canada's "Mr. Enthusiasm"

*B*RIAN LEE CSP

Active as a public speaker from the age of 15 when he completed a Junior Achievement course, Brian Lee CSP has applied his exceptional communications skills in a host of ways.

Becoming successful in business as the Vice-President of a major retail firm by the age of 25, he then entered politics two years later and was elected Calgary's youngest-ever Alderman. Nine productive years in public life on City Council and as a Provincial MLA provided Brian with public speaking opportunities on a daily basis.

Brian Lee's Career Highlights

◆ Brian Lee is a past president of the Canadian Association of Professional Speakers (Alberta Chapter) and past Assistant Area Governor, Toastmasters International as well as past president of the University of Calgary Oxford Debating Society.

◆ Brian Lee CSP is one of North America's leading experts in the field of World-Class Customer Satisfaction and Change Leadership has authored five books.

◆ For two consecutive years, Brian has been evaluated by the International Customer Service Association Conference as the number one rated Customer Service Speaker in the world.

◆ "Mr. Customer Satisfaction" travels over 150,000 miles a year, delivering over 180 keynotes and seminars, and has spoken in every state and province, and 12 countries worldwide.

◆ As both a speaker and implementation consultant to over 100 Fortune 500 corporations and health care organizations, Brian is sought-after as an advisor/coach to senior management, specializing in long-term strategic solutions.

◆ He has been awarded the National Speakers Association Professional Designation, CSP (Certified Speaking Professional), becoming one of less than 20 in Canada, and 500 in the world.

◆ Custom Learning Systems Group Ltd. (CLS) was founded by Brian Lee CSP in 1984. Headquartered in Calgary, Alberta, CLS has offices in Winnipeg and Toronto, and serves its client roster of 6,000 organizations in North America with a team of 24 world-class trainers and communication professionals.

Put Brian Lee to work for your next conference or meeting.
1–800–66–SPEAK (667–7325) • *Keynotes* • *Seminars* • *Consulting* • *Coaching*
(for information, see Customer Responsiveness/Professional Development page 109)

6 Powerful Reasons to Put Brian Lee to Work for You:

☑ 1. Brian Lee is a World-Class Author:
In addition to his busy speaking calendar, Brian brings the credibility of having authored four books:

➤ **Satisfaction Guaranteed™**
How to Satisfy Every Customer Every Time

➤ **Leadership Strategies**
A Leadership Anthology with introduction by F. Lee Bailey

➤ **One Minute Name Memory**
How to Remember Every Name – Every Time – Forever!

➤ **The Wedding MC**
How to MC and Speak at Weddings

Brian also has produced two dozen popular audio and video cassette albums, as well as numerous articles.

☑ 2. Brian Lee Gets Immediate Results:
With a track record of personally speaking to over 750,000 people in the past 19 years as a professional speaker, Brian consistently earns an astonishing audience rating of 4.8 (out of a possible 5). Each year, Brian receives hundreds of letters testifying to the long-term impact and influence he has in the work place and with people's careers.

☑ 3. Brian Lee's Remarkable Customizing Skills are his Trademark:
Every speaking engagement is created from scratch for each new audience.
The quote from Rick Martinez's unsolicited letter (right) is typical of the feedback received from literally hundreds of meeting planners who consistently rave about Brian's unique 37 step process of custom-tailoring and personalizing each and every presentation, right down to the detail of remembering the names of everyone in his audience.

☑ 4. Brian Lee Educates, Empowers, Entertains and Recommends:
Brian is not just a motivational speaker. He is a leading edge, high content educator who enhances his crystal clear delivery skills with a unique combination of sincerity, relevant humour and passion, with step-by-step recommendations for implementation. Put Brian on the platform for you, then get ready to see your people take action.

☑ 5. Brian Lee is a CSP – Certified Speaking Professional
Certified Speaking Professional (CSP) is an earned designation conferred by the National Speakers Association to recognize demonstrated commitment to the speaking profession through proven speaking experience. In 1993, Brian Lee received this prestigious certification. Fewer than 20 speakers in Canada and 500 people in the world have passed the rigorous criteria to attain this coveted designation.

☑ 6. Brian Lee *IS* Canada's "Mr. Enthusiasm"
Brian Lee focuses on the joy that is gained from a job well done. The nickname "Mr. Enthusiasm" wasn't created by a public relations firm, but rather "leapt" from the pages of tens of thousands of audience evaluation forms from Brian's diary of over 2,500 speaking engagements during the past 19 years.

Ⓦ Westinghouse Hanford Company

"I am especially impressed with your ability to grasp the issues we're struggling with at Westinghouse in the nuclear industry and to be able to incorporate them into the seminars. In fact, one Human Resource manager commented, 'I'm embarrassed because Brian knows more about my company than I do.' Your research and homework obviously paid off."

Rick Martinez,
Human Resources Specialist
Westinghouse Hanford Company

112

Brian Lee CSP – Keynote/Seminar Topics

☑ Yes, we may be interested in a Brian Lee CSP presentation on:

A The following topic(s) that are listed in the audio/video/book library listed on pages 117 to 125:

Title(s) _____

_____

B The following topic(s) listed below:

❏ **Feature Conference Keynotes**

- ❏ Thriving on Change
- ❏ Anything You Can Do, You Can Do Better
- ❏ The Six Secrets of People Empowerment
- ❏ The Challenge of Leadership Excellence
- ❏ The Six Secrets of Personal Enthusiasm
- ❏ Reinventing Training
- ❏ Succeed From Adversity
- ❏ Creating Opportunity Through Personal Entrepreneurship

❏ **Customer Satisfaction**

- ❏ The 13 Secrets of Creating World-Class Customer Satisfaction
- ❏ Change Your Culture or Be Doomed to Repeat the Past

❏ **Health Care**

- ❏ The Service Excellence Advisor Train the Trainer Initiative
- ❏ The Challenge of Sustaining and Growing a Medical Practice Through the Year 2000
- ❏ Growing Through Cultural Diversity

❏ **Team Work**

- ❏ Building Self-Empowered Teams
- ❏ Creating High Performance Teamwork with People You Don't Know or Like

❏ **Change Leadership**

- ❏ Take Charge of our Future Change Leadership Summit

❏ **Communication**

- ❏ Communication Dynamics
- ❏ Why People Do What They Do

❏ **Professional Development**

- ❏ The Dynamics of Effective Boards
- ❏ The Power of Professional Development
- ❏ G.O.A.L. Master

❏ **Government**

- ❏ Vision, Values and Empowering Public Sector Leadership
- ❏ S.E.R.V.I.C.E. Your Constituents and Save Your Sanity
- ❏ The Wit and Humour of Politics

113

Brian's Clients Say it Best:

"You now hold the world's record for the greatest number of participants in class for the last session of the conference."

Susan Goewey
Director of Administration – State Government Affairs Council

"The seminar effectively blended values with practical communication skills development. And, in doing so, you re-affirmed and revitalized our staff's commitment to quality service."

Stephen R. Robertson
Director of Human Resources – St. Mary Medical Center

"Energetic, dynamic, informative and interesting. Motivates you about the topic in a manner that makes you want to run out and implement new ideas immediately."

Jim Murphy
City Manager – City of Normandy Park

"In my experience, the memory of most seminars fades within a week or two. The unique thing about your seminar is that six months later, we are still talking about it and still practising the ideas you implemented."

Yasmin Jackson
Manager, Systems and Administration – Bell Canada Int.

"Dynamic, challenging and headed toward the 21st century."

Lawrence Derry
Program Supervisor AADAC – Downtown Treatment Edmonton

"I couldn't have hoped for a more dynamic, focused and useful presentation! 'The Challenge of Municipal Excellence' was one of the best sessions on leadership held during the conference and received consistently high ratings from mayors and council members."

Thomas H. McCloud
Director of Public Affairs – National League of Cities

"Fantastic! Thanks for the superb job... people are still quoting you... and the most complimentary thing being said about you... 'During the whole session my mind never day dreamed to other issues... I kept listening to his every word.'"

Hugo Graff
Plan Manager – Chromalox Inc.

ℛEADER SATISFACTION SURVEY

Brian Lee CSP
Author, *Satisfaction Guaranteed*™

Dear Customer Satisfaction Professional:

This book came about as the result of years of experience combined with suggestions and ideas from hundreds of sources.

Feedback is truly the "breakfast of champions," and your experience, ideas and suggestions will contribute to making this book better for future users.

Accordingly, I would appreciate it if you would share with me your observations by completing the attached Reader Satisfaction Survey.

With thanks in advance,

Brian C. Lee CSP

$\mathcal{R}$EADER SATISFACTION SURVEY

To: **Brian Lee CSP**

Custom Learning Systems Group Ltd.

#200, 2133 Kensington Road N.W.
Calgary, Alberta Canada T2N 3R8
Fax: (403) 228-6776   Email: info@customlearning.com
Web site: www.customlearning.com

From: Name: _____

Address: _____

City: _____

Province/State: _____ P.C./Zip: _____

Bus. Phone: (__)_____ Fax: (__)_____

Email: _____

Re: Comments/Observations – *Satisfaction Guaranteed*™.

1. **The best idea/technique gained and used from the book is:**

_____

_____

_____

2. **Comments, feedback received from Customer or others who have benefited from this book:**

_____

_____

_____

3. **Suggestions for improving existing ideas, content, format:**

_____

_____

_____

READER SATISFACTION SURVEY (CONT.)

4. Suggested "Best Idea" that could be added:

_____

_____

_____

5. I became aware of the book by/through:

_____

_____

_____

6. P.S.

_____

_____

_____

_____

7. On a scale of 1 – 5, *Satisfaction Guaranteed™* was:
   (5 = Valuable, 1 = Poor)

   1. Practical, helpful and relevant   5   4   3   2   1
   2. Well-organized   5   4   3   2   1
   3. Easy to use, reader friendly   5   4   3   2   1
   4. Good value for the money   5   4   3   2   1
   5. *Overall* I rate Satisfaction Guaranteed™ 5   4   3   2   1
   6. What could we do to serve you better?

   _____

   _____

   _____

   _____

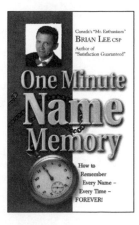

Satisfaction Guaranteed™
by Brian Lee CSP
"Master the Six Secrets of Creating World-Class Customer Satisfaction"
(PB600) **$19.95/29.95**

One Minute Name Memory
by Brian Lee CSP
"How to Remember Every Name – Every Time – Forever!"
(PB1455C) **$24.95**

Wisdom Worth Quoting
by Brian Lee CSP
"52 Certificates Suitable for Framing"
(PB200) **$39.95**

The Wedding M.C.
by Brian Lee CSP
"How to M.C. and Speak at Weddings. A step-by-step guide."
(PB400) **$29.95**

Advanced Presentation Skills
Train the Trainer Course by Brian Lee CSP
"How to Design & Deliver the Best Training
Program of your Life Every Time"

12-Volume Audio Album
(PA2501) **$177.77**

Also Available:
Six-Volume
Video Album
(PV2501) **$195.00**

Advanced Presentation Skills
(APS) Participant Workbook
by Brian Lee CSP
A 250-page manual to accompany the
APS 12-hour course (above).
Learning Guide (W2501) **$95.00**

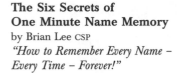

The Six Secrets of One Minute Name Memory
by Brian Lee CSP
"How to Remember Every Name – Every Time – Forever!"

Two-Volume Audio Album
(PA1455C) **$24.95**

Also Available:
One-Video (PV1455C) **$95.00**
Book (PB1455C) **$24.95**

The Genius of Great Audience Participation
by Brian Lee CSP
"How to Empower and Create Audience Ownership"

One-Volume Video Album
(PV2555) **$95.00**

The Wedding M.C.
by Brian Lee CSP
"How to M.C. and Speak at Weddings. A step-by-step guide."
Book (PB400) **$29.95**

Six Star™ Customer Satisfaction Series
by Brian Lee CSP
"Creating World-Class Customer Satisfaction"

12-Volume Audio Album
(PA544A) **$177.77**

6-Volume Video Album
(PV544A) **$595.00**

Individual Six Star Customer Satisfaction Albums

❏ **Satisfaction Guaranteed™**
"How to Create Lifetime Customer Loyalty"
2-Video Set (PV545A) $175.00
2-Audio Set (PA545A) $29.95
16 pg. Workbook (W545A) $3.00
130 pg. Book (PB600) $19.95

❏ **Winning With Difficult Customers**
"How You Can Say to the Most Difficult Customer in the World – Come and Get Me!"
2-Video Set (PV550A) $175.00
2-Audio Set (PA550A) $29.95
16 pg. Workbook (W550A) $3.00

❏ **Stress-Free Service Excellence**
"How to Create a Stress-Free Environment for You and Your Customers"
2-Video Set (PV555A) $175.00
2-Audio Set (PA555A) $29.95
16 pg. Workbook (W555A) $3.00

❏ **One Minute Service Selling**
"How to Gain a Competitive Advantage by Helping Others Get What they Want"
2-Video Set (PV560A) $175.00
2-Audio Set (PA560A) $29.95
16 pg. Workbook (W560A) $3.00

❏ **Managing Moments of Truth**
"How to Continuously Improve Customer Satisfaction"
2-Video Set (PV565A) $175.00
2-Audio Set (PA565A) $29.95
16 pg. Workbook (W565A) $3.00

❏ **Self Esteem & Service Superstars**
"Enhanced Self-Esteem Equals Enhanced Service Excellence"
2-Video Set (PV570A) $175.00
2-Audio Set (PA570A) $29.95
16 pg. Workbook (W570A) $3.00

Brian Lee CSP
"Canada's Mr. Enthusiasm"
presents a *live* video seminar entitled

Service Empowerment Leadership Course

Service Empowerment Leadership Course

Creating a Customer-Driven Culture Through People Empowerment and Continuous Improvement.

Service Empowerment Leadership Course
by Brian Lee CSP
"Creating a Customer-Driven Culture through People Empowerment and Continuous Improvement"

12-Volume Audio Album
(PA2320A) **$177.77**

6-Volume Video Album
(PV2320A) **$595.00**

Individual Service Empowerment Leadership Course Albums

❏ **Vision, Values & Inspired Leadership**
"How to Create a Customer-Driven Culture"
2-Video Set (PV2340A) $175.00
2-Audio Set (PA2340A) $29.95
16 pg. Workbook (W2340A) $3.00

❏ **Thriving on Change**
"How to Survive and Thrive in the Midst of Change"
2-Video Set (PV2345A) $175.00
2-Audio Set (PA2345A) $29.95
16 pg. Workbook (W2345A) $3.00

❏ **The Genius of People Empowerment**
"How to Motivate and Empower for Peak Performance"
2-Video Set (PV2350A) $175.00
2-Audio Set (PA2350A) $29.95
16 pg. Workbook (W2350A) $3.00

❏ **The Power of Continuous Improvement**
"How to Measure and Significantly Improve Customer Perception and Satisfaction"
2-Video Set (PV2355A) $175.00
2-Audio Set (PA2355A) $29.95
16 pg. Workbook (W2355A) $3.00

❏ **Total Quality Leadership**
"How to Implement the 13 Steps of Total Quality Process Improvement"
2-Video Set (PV2360A) $175.00
2-Audio Set (PA2360A) $29.95
16 pg. Workbook (W2360A) $3.00

❏ **The Challenge of Innovative Excellence**
"How to Continuously Improve Service While Creatively Reducing Costs"
2-Video Set (PV2365A) $175.00
2-Audio Set (PA2365A) $29.95
16 pg. Workbook (W2365A) $3.00

**Advanced Professional
S.E.R.V.I.C.E. Selling**
by Brian Lee CSP
*"How to Double Sales Productivity Through
the Seven Values of Sales Mastery"*
12-Audio Album (PA1903) **$197.77**
Learning Guide (W1903) **$95.00**

**Advanced Professional *Auto*
S.E.R.V.I.C.E. Selling**
by Brian Lee CSP
*"How to Double Auto Sales Productivity
Through the 7 Values of Sales Mastery"*
24-Audio Album (PA1903AUTO) **$295.00**
Learning Guide (W1903AUTO) **$95.00**

**The Six Secrets of Sales
Empowerment**
by Brian Lee CSP
*"How to Recruit, Hire, Motivate and
Empower Peak Sales Performance"*
One-Volume Video Album
(PV472H) **$175.00**

**Trade Show Marketing
Effectiveness**
by Brian Lee CSP
*"Trade Show Marketing Strategies For
Planning, Selling and Exhibiting Success"*
Six-Volume Audio Album
(PA2480) **$89.95**

1-800-66-Speak
www.customlearning.com

Reinventing Sales &
Marketing in a Professional
Services Practice
by Brian Lee CSP
*"How to Achieve a Long-Term
Competitive Advantage by
Creating a Customer-Driven,
Sales Focused Culture"*
Six-Volume Audio Album
(PA1909) **$89.95**

Telemarketing Sales &
Communication Effectiveness
by Brian Lee CSP
*"How to Achieve Extraordinary, Cost-
Effective Results through Sales and
Communication Mastery"*
Six-Volume Audio Album
(PA1450) **$89.95**

The Six Secrets of Networking
& Highly Effective Business
Marketing
by Brian Lee CSP
*"How to Transform Informal
Contacts into Unlimited Business
and Social Opportunities"*
One-Volume Video Album
(PV471G) **$149.95**

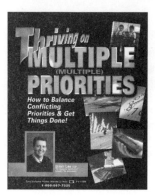

Thriving on Multiple (Multiple) Priorities
by Brian Lee CSP
"How to Balance Conflicting Priorities & Get Things Done"

Two-Volume Video Album
(PV1786) **$175.00**

Four-Volume Audio Album
(PA1782) **$69.95**

The 7 Attributes of Meeting Mastery
by Brian Lee CSP
"How to Organize the Best Meeting of Your Life Everytime"

Four-Volume Audio Album
(PA2742A) **$69.95**

Stress Master
by Brian Lee CSP
"How to Survive and Thrive in Spite of Stress & Fatigue"

Six-Volume Audio Album
(PA1776) **$89.95**

Winning with Difficult People
by Brian Lee CSP
"How You Can Say to the Most Difficult People in the World... Come and Get Me"

Two-Volume Video Album
(PV1793) **$195.00**

Six-Volume Audio Album
(PA1793) **$89.95**

The 13 Secrets of Creating World-Class Customer Satisfaction
by Brian Lee CSP
"How to Create a Customer-Driven Culture Through People Empowerment & Continuous Improvement"

One-Volume Video Album
(PV481) **$95.95**

Anything You Can Do... You Can Do Better
by Brian Lee CSP
"How to Put the Power of Excellence to Work in Your Professional Career & Personal Life"

Two-Volume Audio Album
(PA408E) **$24.95**

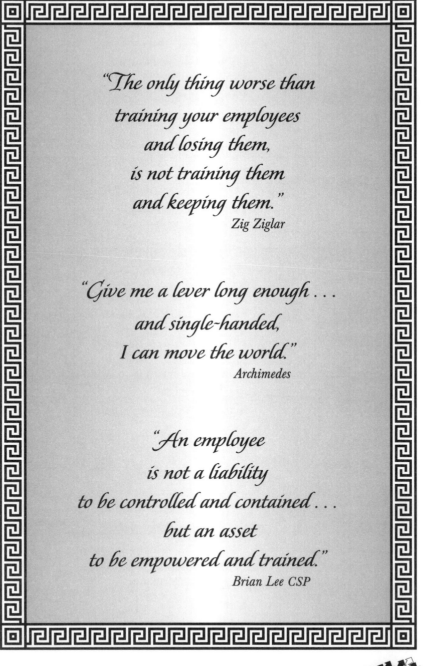

"The only thing worse than
training your employees
and losing them,
is not training them
and keeping them."
Zig Ziglar

"Give me a lever long enough . . .
and single-handed,
I can move the world."
Archimedes

"An employee
is not a liability
to be controlled and contained . . .
but an asset
to be empowered and trained."
Brian Lee CSP

1-800-66-Speak
www.customlearning.com

$\mathcal{P}$RODUCT ORDER FORM

Order by:

Name:_____ Title: _____
Organization:_____
Address:_____
City: _____ State/Prov.: _____
Country:_____ Zip/P.C.: _____
Daytime Phone: _____ Fax: _____
Email: _____

Ship to: (if different from above)

Name:_____ Title: _____
Organization: _____
Address:_____
City: _____ State/Prov.: _____
Country: _____ Zip/P.C.: _____
Daytime Phone: _____ Fax: _____

Order:

Quantity	Title	Order Number	Audio	Video	Other	Unit Price	Total

Merchandise Total	
Shipping & Handling	
Sub-Total	
G.S.T.	
GRAND TOTAL	

Shipping & Handling

$ 0 – $ 50	$ 8.95	$151 – $200	$11.95
$ 51 – $100	$ 9.95	$201 – $250	$12.95
$101 – $150	$10.95	$251 – $300	$13.95

For orders totalling over $300, add $1 for each additional $50 of purchases.

Method of Payment

❑ Cheque #

Made payable to:

Custom Learning Systems Group Ltd.
#200, 2133 Kensington Road N.W.
Calgary, Alberta T2N 3R8
Fax: (403) 228-6776
Toll Free: 1-800-667-7325

❑ Charge to
  ❑ MasterCard
  ❑ Visa

Card #:_____

Expiry: _____

Cardholder
Signature: _____

1-800-66-Speak
www.customlearning.com   129

To purchase additional copies of this book, please
visit our secure online store at:

www.customlearning.com/estore/

Other products available
in our online store:

*"One Minute Name Memory:
How to Remember Every Name, Every Time...Forever!"*
book

"6 Secrets to Personal Enthusiasm"
1 audio CD

"13 Secrets of World Class Customer Satisfaction"
video

"Inspiration, Enthusiasm & Teamwork"
10 CD audio set

"Keep Your Nurses and Healthcare Professionals for Life™"
book, 4 CD audio set

*"Essential Strategies to Become the
HealthCare Employer of Choice"*
4 CD audio set